Instructions for a Flood

Caitlin Press Inc.
3375 Ponderosa Way
Qualicum Beach, BC V9K 2J8
caitlinpress.com

Text and cover design by Vici Johnstone
Map and illustrations by Chrissy Courtney
Cover image by Suzo Hickey
Printed in Canada

Caitlin Press Inc. acknowledges financial support from the Government of Canada and the Canada Council for the Arts, and the Province of British Columbia through the British Columbia Arts Council and the Book Publisher's Tax Credit.

Library and Archives Canada Cataloguing in Publication

Title: Instructions for a flood : reflections on story, geography and connection / Adrienne Fitzpatrick.
Names: Fitzpatrick, Adrienne, 1966- author.
Description: Essays.
Identifiers: Canadiana 20230156657 | ISBN 9781773861128 (softcover)
Classification: LCC PS8611.I89 I57 2023 | DDC C814/.6—dc23

INSTRUCTIONS
FOR A FLOOD

Reflections on Story, Geography and Connection

Adrienne
Fitzpatrick

CAITLIN PRESS 2023

In memory of Kelly Posthuma, the purveyor of experience.

Contents

1

2

3

4

5

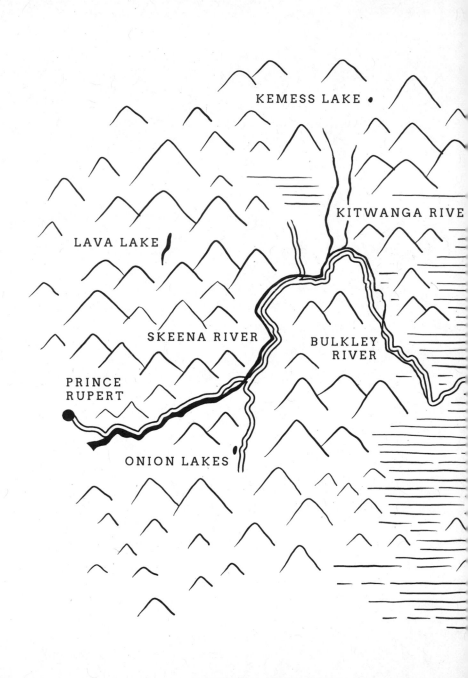

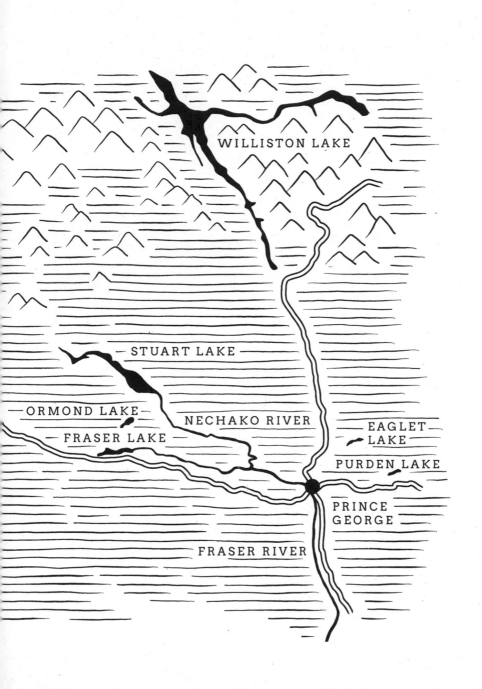

1

Blackwater Road

Blackwater Road

A place you drive through on the way somewhere, Vanderhoof is named after a Dutch settler who wanted to build a community for retired writers and attracted over the years various religious factions such as Mennonites, Pennsylvania Dutch and Mormons, along with a staunch Catholic contingent, as if they were drawn by the romantic idea. As if writers ever retire. At the grocery store I would see families in handmade clothes, tall and sturdy women swathed in sensible dresses and black shoes. Nets carefully placed on their plaited hair. Their children would follow them like ducklings, as if they shared the same mind. Like my family, they had faith in the west and their own ideas. Little town tucked away in a narrow valley left behind by the ice age a perfect place to hide out.

In class, we learned about the geography of the BC interior, how it was once the bottom of an ancient glacial lake. Coast Mountains to the west, Rockies rise to the east like a magic kingdom. Desert areas to the south, jagged mountains and tundra to the north. The interior is like the palm of your hand, marked up and lined like old skin, our teacher said. Holding his hand up to us to make his point. Pocked with lakes, rivers, clearings and salt licks. Burn spots and smokestacks, carefully drawn squares of cultivated earth, then wooded and wild, an odd patchwork. Plumes of smog circle up in the central city. Mainly the land is ironed out with a few bumps, shards of stubborn rock left from the last ice age that scraped the middle clean. Now we live on the crust of a glacial lake, ooze just beneath us. You can see where the waterline was in some places, lip of land and then the stark cut banks where the water dropped off. Banks of the Nechako are like that. Glaciers have left behind a cool silence, blue and hard in the winter, green and swollen in the summer.

Nechako is the river that formed me. Rivers can do that, insert themselves like a body part. Nechako is not what it once was. Dam in the 1950s reduced it to half, choking stream beds flickering with fish. Indigenous bodies that were buried for centuries became unearthed, washed up on shores far from home. It still happens when there is a flood, thin bones slip through to surface, up from the bottom. Ancient sturgeon, scaly with years of hiding, still lurk in dark hollows. Dull dinosaur eyes. Some grow to be the size of dolphins.

Story of our clan and how we got here: My uncle got curious, hearing about opportunities in the west. Restless man, nervous energy flashing through his shrewd eyes. Beckoning of the land beyond the Rockies. Industry building fast, land to be bought, developed, making a go of something new, leave behind the dusty prairies. Generations there bought and sold farms, machinery, built communities over hard distances, drought, blizzard, bulging rivers. He had an idea to start a business, which spread to my father, his little brother, and they took the train, undulating thunk and whir, with me forming, not yet out in the world but motion part of my inheritance. A business bloomed and failed, our name in red block letters on a building in the centre of town replaced by a 7-Eleven, clan members spread out again.

In the summer of 1980, a boy in my school drowned in a little red Camaro. It flipped upside down in a small creek and he couldn't get out. Window open, the cold water rising. He was sixteen, like me, brand new licence, working on the farm to buy the car off his dad. In the soup aisle at the grocery store, I heard Mr. Miller say to Mr. Albertson, All my sons learned to drive tractor when they were fourteen. Rough, splotchy face from all that wind. Curved ball cap sitting on the back of his head. Mr. Albertson said, hands resting on his shopping cart, Coulda happened to any of us.

It makes no sense, said Sandy at the gas station, her blond hair stacked in carefully pinned curls. Mrs. Martin, cashier at the drugstore, stricken face, shaking her head in disbelief. Lineups growing as she recounted the story to each customer. Peter flipped the car in early spring, when warm days mixed with snow, melting creeks, rivers cold and surging. His inexperience didn't help, my dad said. A pall cast over the town, sludgy like the effluence that floated on the river, down from the old mill.

Post office was where all notices went: weddings, reunions, job ads. Funerals with withered pale faces, stalwarts that helped raise up the town. Then the notice for Peter's funeral was taped on the glass doors. Beaming face, dancing brown eyes greeting everyone who passed through. Lips parted like he was about to speak. Our principal said that anyone who wanted to go to the funeral could take the afternoon off, with the permission of parents. I didn't know Peter well, but mainly I didn't want to see his body. Everyone said it was going to be open casket.

Students would go to the accident scene, whisper about the wrecked guardrail on the bridge, how the tow rope scratched the road like sharp fingernails. Lure of accidents like a drug. People slowing on the highway past a car in the ditch, flare of police lights, screaming sirens. How is it always someone else, and not you?

When I got my licence, I would go for drives in the spring evenings or early mornings on the weekend. Blackwater Road runs past the bright white and brown sign to West Lake, a well-used provincial park. For Sale signs with pictures of eager real estate agents sway on the side of the road. Sharp left and right, past a row of mailboxes, sun dapples the pavement, past the boat launch turnoff to the public beach site. Enormous parking lot, dusty, concrete ties marking off rows, already half-full. During the day it's crowded with moms and young kids. Teenagers come after school; you can hear them wheel in, music booming. I walk along the paved walk, past rows of polished picnic tables, find a spot under a tree close to a bridge over a tiny creek. One spring day, a bear wandered across it, dazed and hungry after its long sleep. People yelled but it hovered at the edge of the beach. Some people left; others ignored it and stayed. Eventually it crossed back.

Lake is wide and bends to the left, can't see how far it goes. There are big houses with immaculate docks, boats quietly tied. Sea-Doos rip down the centre, and in the shallows little children squabble over floaties. An eagle has a nest at the top of a tree next to me; I can see droppings like splattered paint, and no one settles there. In the evening, when the train rolls through, coyotes howl and yip from just beyond the treeline. Wild chorus, close and chilling. You can hear the pups wailing. Maybe their eyes are fastened on us, waiting for an opportunity.

The water is colder than I expect, stained rust from the tree tannins. Bottom is gravel with sharp stones and I totter and lunge until my arms spread out, flicking the surface. Fish graze my calves, weeds tangle in my toes. Beach is knotted with legs and faces, undulating arms. I walk out to the black line of the drop-off, my toes feeling the crumbling edge. A young boy with a snorkel hunches face down to see, arms swirling and then thrashing as his shoulders, then his little body submerge, losing balance. His father rushes over to him as he struggles to his feet. Dumdum lake, he cries with his first breath, sputtering water. Inconsolable, his wails punctuate the air, his face red, fists clenched. I learned to swim at this beach when I was ten; we all learned here since there was no swimming pool. Five girls standing in the shallow part of the river where the current ebbed, safe enough for us to submerge. It was always cold; unrelenting shivering. Maybe it was fear. We learned some basic strokes, how to float, all of us flailing. Final test was to submerge, hold your breath and swim a few strokes. I opened my eyes underwater, a few of us did, on a dare, to get a glimpse of the murky world. Cold water entering my eyes like a portal, as if they were an entryway and not a barrier. Some weeds, ripple of sand, nothing alive that I could see. But life was all around, I knew, and death. One girl, Loretta, with curly red hair, squealed, saying she felt the fin of a fish brush her leg, as if in greeting, her face flushed in the telling. One girl could not do it, Evelyn; tiny and determined, no matter how much the instructor encouraged her, she would only bend her head back and let the water stroke her short, dark hair. She would not even take off her glasses.

Blackwater Road, past thirty kilometres, crumbles to dirt, goes all the way to Quesnel if you're in the mood to wander. You feel like that sometimes. Road threads through hills, sprinkled with green stems. All the land spread out, swamp here, curve there; very few cars. After a few kilometres, it all looks the same and your mind latches to a blue patch of sky up ahead; you follow it like a beacon. It starts out paved, swinging past trailers with additions, expansive fields and tidy farmhouses. Horses plod on trails by the road, ATVs whining through the open window; country roads sprawl off like crooked tree limbs.

Blackwater Road slows through a recovery centre for alcoholics and drug addicts. It looks like an army barracks with its small, neat buildings, white trimmed windows. I didn't see anyone when I went through and I imagined bodies sweaty and suffering in beds, bodies slouched in upright chairs, circling a droning voice coaxing them back to life. Past the recovery centre, road runs into gravel and logging radio signals are pounded on slim trees. Country roads change to spurs, rough hems and lumpy with potholes. No homes or houses, just trees being hacked and hauled.

MacKenzie Lake, announced by a large, greyish-green sign, pounded high up an aspen tree at Mile 8. I turn left and ease my wheels through the deep holes. Narrow road dusty with white clay: only room for one car going in, one car coming out. Road switchbacks down a steep incline, past two weathered picnic tables in tiny gravel landings, and I'm at the edge. Small and weedy; I can see the far side where skinny poplars grow right up to the shore, their tips reflecting on the water skein, pointing at me. A few mallards scurry off in unison as I approach. Nothing seems to move.

No one knows where I am, a sudden realization, uncomfortable fact. I think about the people who have come here, families with small children, maybe teenagers coming to party. There is no beach to loll on, but the remoteness is appealing. No one to complain if the music roars, the children cry. This is the place where things and people are discarded, between paved and gravel, smooth and stony. Phone reception gone; only the lake and the trees witness my presence. I didn't stay to feel the water, but I could sense the bottom. The part of me that is hidden comes crawling up my neck as I hurry to my car; slowly see-sawing through the rough holes, hoping to avoid a faceoff with a car making its way down to the shore. Gravel turns to pavement, wild sprawling forest recedes, then disappears, replaced by fences holding in livestock, keeping out predators, hungry coyotes, wolves. Signs for West Lake pass, cars pulling in and out at the turnoff. Heads bobbing to music.

Day of the funeral and Mom said I could go but I wavered. In the end Anna convinced me, grabbed me by the arm and we joined the crowd going to the church. Whole town is going, she said. Wouldn't do if you missed it. Hearse was already parked outside, black opaque windows like bug eyes. I held my breath as we walked past, like something inside could hear me, darkness reaching out to touch us. All the pews at the front were packed and there were rows of wooden chairs behind them. We slipped into a row. High school music teacher playing the piano, her husband strumming guitar. Casket open at the front, sheen of the brown wood glowing in the afternoon light. I could see the soft white interior when we stood to sing.

Peter's parents and brother were in the front row; I could see the backs of their bowed heads. Light flooded through the long windows and the brightness refracted through the room, shards of it resting on our shoulders. I sang the hymns I knew and mumbled the ones I didn't. An offertory basket was passed, brimming with money for the family, some envelopes with notes stuffed in with kind words. Smell of incense infused the air, a haze drifting with the dust motes. Muffled sobs, cry of babies. Then we stood to walk past the casket to pay our respects and leave.

In the little prairie town where my father grew up, they had wakes in houses. A tradition carried over from the old country, still flowing through their veins. In Ireland, he told me, when someone died, or if people thought a person was dying, they would call family and friends over. People would eat, drink and debate in the next room. Disagreements about politics, past resentments, stories of the person they were waiting on. Women would take turns sitting with the body, so they could be there in case the person woke up. They could hear if there were any last words from open lips. *Death is nothing at all. It does not count,* my father would say, from a poem he had heard at wakes. *I have only slipped away into the next room. Everything remains as it was.* Because death can look like slumber. That's what I thought when I passed by Peter, his calm smooth face, brown hair perfectly arranged. His lips parted but silent. Hands clasped in a way that he never would have done in life, still as snow.

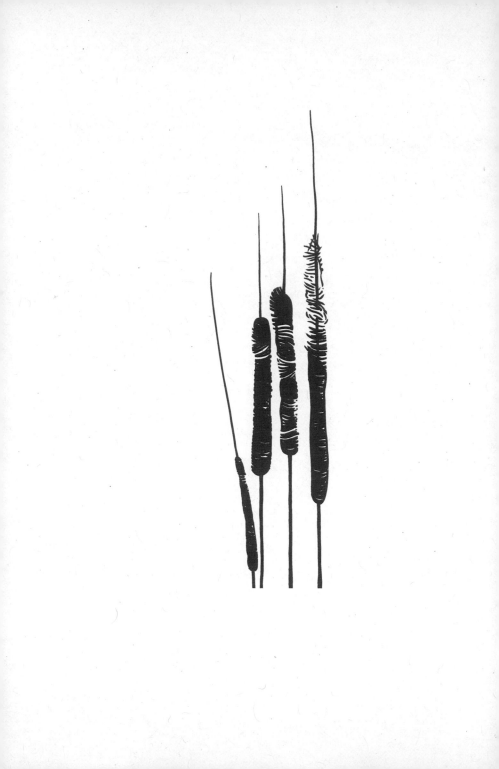

2

Purden Lake
Mud River
Eaglet Lake
Fraser River Headwaters

Purden Lake

It is Taylor's birthday, hot beginning of July. We eat a skillet breakfast at Denny's, my treat, and a young burly man beside us has a booth to himself, bent over his sketch pad. Taylor steals a quick glance. He's drawing a dragon but not the Disney kind, she says. More Japanese. Majestic neck and intricate scales. I think I saw some fire coming out of its nose. Maybe he'll give it to you as a present if you ask nice, I say. His forearms are thick, fair skin mottled with tattoos. Nah, I already have a dragon, she answers as we push out the front doors, heat rifling through the space between us.

Taylor has never been to Purden Lake, so we pack up some water, snacks and coolers in my SUV and head east. The day is ours, I declare as I crank music, AC. Lake is on the road to Jasper; rugged and lonely, even in the summer it seems unused, as if we are encountering the outer edges of an abandoned land. Open road unfolds over steep hills; from the top glimpses of the Rockies jut blue and pink in the light.

My mom used to drop us off at the lake near our house and let our older brothers look after my sister and me, Taylor says. They took off with their friends and we sat under a tree, waiting and watching kids play, she adds, twirling her hair with a red polished nail.

Parking lot is mostly full. We nab the last bit of nubby grass, next to some lounging teenagers. They are pale and sullen, even in the brightness, wearing shorts past their knees as if to ward off the heat. Little round bellies flare out when they reach for a beer. Lake like a bucket, round and deep at the base of a ski hill. You can see the switchbacks of trails, carved criss-crosses. Lake ringed with peaks, small cabins perched on the other side.

I love beaches, they are like the starting line to the deliciousness of lakes, I say, especially beaches up north. This isn't up north, Taylor says, swats me with her hat. This is the middle, the centre, where people pass through on their way up to somewhere else.

I lie out flat, sprayed and slopped with sunscreen. Lolling my head to the side, anticipating the moment when the sun pokes and kneads through the knots in my neck, my back, when I start to melt and feel a primal connection to the earth. When the heat is too much, a dip in the clear cold water is bracing, knocks the sleepy heat out of my body. Wade up to my neck, let the shock of it penetrate even further through. Then I repeat, as much and as often as I can stand it. I swear you are an iguana, Taylor says, throws back her thick hair, her clunky earrings glinting. Beaches where I grew up were packed with tourists, felt like they weren't even ours. We had to get there early and fight for space like everyone else. Taylor and I found each other, an instant recognition, like picking someone out of a lineup. A face, a look you recognize but you don't know where from. Her intensity unnerved me but then I grew accustomed to the energy that could go anywhere. We would get into a car together to get some lunch and end up buying crystal balls at a shop with a blind resident dog.

Kids were stalking minnows with nets and buckets, the youngest ones squealing when the tiny fish got so close to their feet, then swerved. Delighted at how they moved in an instant, seemed to have one mind, an electric connection. People aren't like minnows, Taylor says with a wry smile. They go all over the place, don't pay attention to signs, don't trust a leader. We laugh and drink deeply from our coolers, trying not to splash our faces.

Taylor gets up to test the water, wade in knee deep and watch the black tadpoles that hatch by the thousands at places like Purden Lake. Sun washing the lake, her face white and sweaty, a thinly painted sheen, and then it goes slack with shock. There are so many tadpoles, little slivers of life, and the kids with their buckets eagerly capture them and haul them up to shore. Taylor comes over to me, concerned: if the tadpoles can't swim, they'll die. I look over at the lounging moms, chatting, juggling food and phones, the buckets forgotten in favour of lunch. Taylor strides over and explains the tadpole predicament to the mothers. The little kids walk down to the beach and empty the buckets, eyes cast down, and quickly run back to their moms.

Here's to the tadpoles. May they live long and happy lives. We cheer each other when Taylor returns. Beach is bursting now, all the picnic tables are claimed, rickety chairs unfolded, sunglasses, hats, books. There is chatter, faint music, bodies turning over and over so the sun can reach everywhere. I walk in up to my neck, feel the sharp stones on the bottom that throw me. Water clear, mountain cold; I relish the shiver that creeps up my skull, the full immersion, spreading out all my limbs and letting the sky hold me in place.

Mud River

If you want to go tubing, Mud River's the place, Franca calls out from the back seat, over the radio, while Taylor looks for a bottle opener in her purse. Franca came here as a teenager herself, so she knows all about it. I catch her in the rear-view mirror, blond hair grazing her shoulders, sun hat pulled low. You'll be our tour guide, I say to her, and she says, There's not much to see. Mud, beaches, beer cans and white bellies. I've never been there but I've passed traffic turning off down the dusty road, spotted bare arms and legs bobbing just past the bridge. Major teenager hangout, reeks of pot; thankfully they go off in the bush for their make-out sessions, Franca says as we follow a white F-150 down to the tiny parking lot. All dust and huge holes you have to swerve around quick, squeeze in beside some bushes, out of the afternoon sun.

Patches of young moms are spread out close to the bridge, their toddlers squealing along the bumpy shore, little fists clenched with dirt. River's a tight S shape, sloping over exposed gravel beds that feel cool and soothing on my feet.

We walk past the moms and out on the gravel bed and the river sweeps to the right. Think there is a nice beach around the corner, Taylor says, just not sure how we get there. We start climbing exposed tree roots on the shore that turn to crumbling cliffs, so we backtrack. We can walk across the river at a narrow point, Franca points out. There are other people crossing, bags and coolers balanced on their heads, water swirling around their shoulders, so we follow them. Mud River is skinny but I have to focus on keeping my feet on the rippled bottom. It doesn't look like much, but it can knock out your knees like a sucker punch.

People don't come here to swim, just hang out, Taylor says. Glamorous scarf wraps her long dark hair, Jackie O glasses and cut-off jeans. We stretch out on a hump of the S, facing hollowed-out overhangs. A purple-haired girl and her boyfriend walk past; he is clad in jeans with chains draped around his slim hips. They saunter around the corner, off to their secret lair. Sound of rap music, angry voice cutting through the heat, rush of water. Small stones on the beach push through taut muscles in my back, little pockets like liquid heat. I inch down to the river and slide in crablike, easing in my legs, sweaty middle and up to my neck, my arms anchored on the shore. Letting the muddy water braid through me, power of the current lifting my legs up; lean my head back, let my hair drift through.

Water draws me in, just so far, pressure of current forcing my body to resist. Bottom on the verge of slipping, you have to hold on. The pull a kind of testing or teasing, luring me up to the line where the river takes over, underneath pulling like a magnet. You can sense it like a storm coming, a drop in temperature, a cold spread of knowing at the back of your neck. I repeat my slow foray into the river and out. I can see why they call this Mud River, I call out to Taylor and Franca, but they are chatting, lithe and feline on their blankets, and don't hear me as a teenage boy does a screaming cannonball off a crumbling cliff, landing flat on his butt as his friends howl and applaud.

When I flop down on my blanket, Franca is talking about a friend of hers who flew a helicopter over this area, following the squiggly river like bent wire past farms, swamps, ramshackle trailers and elegant homes tucked behind a copse of trees like mushrooms in a field. Hodgepodge of the north, all mixed up and in together, connected by the extreme weather. It matters who your neighbours are—they may dig you out of the ditch, tow you to the shop.

I swear it's like bodysurfing out there, I tell Taylor and Franca, but they don't join me. They find pretty rocks, explore around the S corner and come back giggling. They caught the sultry teen couple nude, tattoos all over them, Taylor says. All you could see were their sweet faces.

I don't want to go but Franca has had enough heat, her face pink and puffy. We walk across the river at the same spot but it feels deeper, water colder than when we arrived. Clothes piled on our heads, unbalanced, unglamorous, current tripping us up. In some countries they do this with grace; rivers and creeks are highways, I say as we reach the shore. No staggering around with sunscreen tubes and empty beer bottles in their bags.

We are spent, filled up with sun and the rancorous river. Minivans are filling up with small children, whimpering in their buckled seats. Moms impatiently slam the doors shut. Go fuck yourself, yells a young woman at her boyfriend across the front seat of a truck. Arms crossed, her brown hair piled in a sloppy bun. Go fuck yourself, he yells back. We sidle past and into my car. Good time to leave, I think, Franca says. Nice day at the beach, Taylor says, and we ease out, trucks and cars with booming music passing us on the way in, honking for more space.

Eaglet Lake

Giscome was a bustling, active community that has since closed its school and sawmill; hard to imagine its heyday as we drive by vacant windows staring out at the doldrums of the road. People still hang in and farm, it's still a vibrant community, Lena says. They have each other's backs, like a lot of small places, Lena tells me. Winding road weaves through the old town on the way to Eaglet Lake. Small and quiet, shaped like a squashed kidney bean. Views of the Rockies to the east; you can see them float on the horizon when you're in the middle of the lake, drifting in a kayak, a canoe. There is a day park, a few picnic tables in a cleared area just off the road; little pull-ins and private spots with rocky beaches, they go quick. We leave early and claim the last one, spread out the blankets, unfold like spring leaves. Lena brings Dixie out of her bag and she scampers to the lake edge and runs back.

Lena smiles, scoops up the tiny floppy white-haired puppy and wades in. Dixie whimpers and tries to scramble up her shoulder. Lena sinks in, her blond hair swept up in a bun, a '50s vision of a beach babe. Dixie's fur floats up to her chin and she frantically paddles in circles when Lena lets her go. I follow her in. Bottom of the lake is mucky and the algae puffs a greenish halo. Clay oozes between my toes. Sense of sinking, that the bottom could give way, that you could go deeper instead of farther.

Road runs one edge of the lake, follows the close curves. Logging trucks chug by; I can see the top layer of skinny logs bouncing. On the other side is the railroad tugging goods from Prince Rupert. Sound of the screech of brakes and then the deep rumble of movement accompanies the day, augments the quiet. Lena drifts farther out to do a few lazy strokes. She kayaks out here often on her own, feels like she owns the whole lake.

Lena and I walked down a country road not far from here, gravel driveways leading off to homesteads hidden by trees. Road was off the highway to the airport. We'd walked down it many times. A black truck with white trim, the body jacked up way past the giant tires, drove past us once, twice, three times and the fourth time it stopped just past us, threatening silence, like a trigger was about to be pulled, waiting for the explosion. Sense of threat in the air. Should we run for it? Who knows who is in that truck, could be a whole crew, I say to Lena. Fields with wooden fences to our left the quickest escape. The driver—I could not see his face, just his shaggy hair—waiting there for excruciating minutes before moving on.

When we got back to her house, we tried to shake it off, that feeling of invasion. Should have got his licence plate, should have called him in. Some faceless creep stalking us on a country road. Maybe we can burn our clothes, never walk down that road again. We drink wine instead, build a fire. I spent the night in her spare room with the single bed, thick comforter, and in the morning spotted a coyote skulking in the field.

Fraser River Headwaters

At dusk we build a fire in the backyard. Expanse of green claimed from the forest, land that requires constant care. Trying to keep the wild out but they keep coming in, Greta says, laughing, waving her hands like she's trying to shoo them away. Meeting a bear on the way to the woodshed. Pack rat taking up residence in the garage. Stubborn presences startling Jim and Greta but they are at peace. We are with them and they are with us, Greta says at the fire. They built their home on the side of a mountain, tucked in close to the end of the Rockies. If you continue east, mountains climb and scratch the sky, rough-hewn faces stark and wrinkled. Shocking and majestic. Busloads come from Japan, Belgium, Amsterdam for the views but here the Rockies wind down, life quietly nestled but still teeming. At night it is so dark that the quiet is like a hum that sings you to sleep.

Yard is festooned with radiant orange rhododendrons, flocks of bursting irises, stalks of verdant flowers the bees feed on. They are so busy tucking in and out of silky pods, they fly around us as if in a drunken haze. So intent and buzzing, keeping the hive going. In the mornings we hang out in patches of sun, Greta, Jim and Zane smoking cigarettes, smoking pot, as we plan out our day. Trip to Small River to fish one day, feasted on by bugs. So many bugs we all had nets over our faces, every part of our bodies covered and sweating. It's July and muggy as hell, so much rain everyone has given up complaining. River so high we are slipping off the muddy banks. We don't last long at the river, running to the safety of the truck, five minutes spent smashing mosquitoes against the windshield with annoyance, until they are finally all dead.

Trip to Kinbasket Lake the next day, man-made lake carved

from a blown-out river valley claimed for hydroelectric power. Jagged peaks bearing down on us, stern as judges. Every rec site we go to is packed, lake so high there is no beach to make a fire on, roast our lunch. We travel to the end of the lake where the road narrows to a pocked trail and we find a spot. Wind froths the lake into iced edges but Zane and his son jump in, unfazed, shivering by the fire. No beach here either. Logs and branches and stumps wash in like refuse from a war. Flood has taken the peace from the lake, left detritus that no one knows what to do with. People use their boats at their own risk here, Greta says. So much drowned life popping up, years later. Unexpected tree could come up right through your bow like a spear. She shows us the river that got swallowed up on the way back, flowing lazy under a wood bridge. Kinbasket bloating around the corner. Whole valley gone now, even the memories of what was there before, ancient stories dying off, maybe some pictures in a museum, grey and fading.

At the fire we don't talk about that. Jim and Greta lived in little cabins for years in the woods and they will never leave. Fire cracks and gathers us in. Zane's son lights fireworks and they blast off into the circle of sky, sounding like trucks backfiring, emitting glittery purple and gold sprinkles. Smoke hazes the stars and then clears. Swirl of galaxies stretching out to infinity from where we stand, so small in the patch of forest the gods could pass right over us.

Every summer for a long time, Greta and I canoed the Fraser at its headwaters, clear and cold as hell, not far from here, Jim says to Zane. They are talking about canoes, which are the lightest, toughest, able to take the currents. Greta and Jim stand close to the fire, leaning into each other, flames dancing in their eyes. They met as teenagers in Jasper when she was travelling from Sweden. They went on a trip to Vancouver together and haven't been apart since. They are close to sixty, exuberant about the place they live in, their oasis in the woods. Passing smokes and joints between them, the story goes back and forth in lobbying lines. It was the same crew every year, Greta says to us. Right then, an owl starts calling out to the night in its plaintive hoots. So rare to hear that, Greta says, her white hair a smooth sheet down the sides of her impish face. Around here they say that owls are the voices of the dead. She flicks her butt into the fire. So is that a warning or a friendly hello? I ask. Could be either or both, nothing to worry about, she says. It's not often we hear them out here, but the dead are always near.

The crew we go with are experienced, Jim says, picking up the thread of the story. Evenings go like this around the fire, after the day's adventure, stories and the dark and the forest leaning in to remind us of things. Going off on tangents, fire drawing us back. And we took lessons, got all the gear, it was hard work but so much fun, Greta says. We'd have a big bonfire on the beach, Jim says, and feast and drink and watch the sun set. It was a ritual we looked forward to, a whole community thing. We'd see people that we wouldn't see for the rest of the year. Jim waves his hands above his head, exclaiming to the night, to us. Yeah, it was great, Greta says, smiling. Their cat Smudge comes out from the dark, darts in between their legs and flies off into the edges of the woods. Zane whittles a stick for marshmallows beside me, his steady hands scraping bark down to the pale wood. Smells of a tart green, like apples.

Then this one trip a few years back, Jim says. There was a logjam up ahead but the canoes ahead of us were getting past it. We could see it coming, Greta and I and Jerry, our friend in the canoe with us. We talked a bit about not going ahead. The turn was tight; coming around a bend full speed, we'd have to paddle really hard to miss the pileup. But we thought we could do it. Our friends had already got past the logjam, were pulling up their canoes on the beach, watching and waiting for the rest of us to come. It was the final stretch.

So we go for it, current's really rough, we're bouncing, we're flying, and the water was so cold. Splashing our faces. I was at the front and I could hardly see, Jim recalls, his voice rising as we all go quiet. Even the owl. Greta gazes at the fire. And we come around the bend so fast, Jim says, and we don't make the corner. I'm up front and I'm screaming. We're heading straight for the logjam and then we all go under.

When I came up the first time my head hit a log, Greta says, speaking to the fire like it will answer her. I couldn't find a space to break through. Current was so strong, I had to hang on hard until I could finally haul myself up. It took all my strength. Water so cold I couldn't feel my body. And I saw Jerry up in the logs but no Jim.

Jim lights a smoke. White of his beard glowing in the fire. Brown eyes taking Zane and me in, holding us like the current did. When I finally haul myself through to breathe, Jim says, I don't have the strength to pull myself out. It takes all I have just to hang on, not let the river carry me away.

Our friends on the beach come to rescue us, swinging ropes from their canoe for us to grab so they can haul us out, Jim says. They get Jerry and Greta; they're both on top of the logjam by then. But I'm still in the water, hanging on, hanging on. I think I'm going to die. I think this is it. Water is so cold, current is so strong. I don't have the strength to grab the rope, I think, and the river will have me.

Greta's face falls then, seems to sink. Fire has died down but no one moves to stoke it.

They swing the rope out and miss me, Jim says, making a swinging motion with his whole body, and then they swing again, and I grab it and I'm screaming when they finally haul me out. Jim's face is grey. When I get to the beach, he says, Greta and Jerry and everyone is there and they take all our clothes off because we're freezing, if we don't get warm we'll die, and we stand by the fire for hours. We're crying, all of us. It took so long to get warm. It was like dying and being reborn, all at once.

And we never went back, Greta says. The night took over then.

3

Fraser Lake
Ormond Lake
Stuart Lake
Lower Road
Red Car

Fraser Lake

Best time to go to Fraser Lake is the winter when the ice is thick and the cold wind has blown the biggest drifts of snow off the lake; it creates a path. Ice is milky but clear in spots, so you can make out fronds of weeds if you look close enough. Ken and I drive out for the afternoon, bring some smokies to roast and some spicy Caesars in a can and walk straight out on the lake. The dogs race ahead and behind, excited by the space. The black Lab chases after every smell; Milo stops often to chew on the snow packed in his paws. Day is bright and cold and clear; you can see every branch sway in the breeze, watch mists of snow sprinkle.

We walk as far as we feel the ice is safe; snow machine tracks jut like ribs, our feet slide over them. Imposing house built on the hill to the north is obvious and ugly; all the other shacky cabins blend in, seamless with the rocks on the shore. Shambling places with rough linoleum and small wood stoves. In the summer the beach is booming, party music, barbecues, campfires that last all night. Quarrels that were brewing in tight quarters in the winter are aired out, full volume and theatrics. Some nights it is us. I'm going to leave her, Larry says at the campfire, full of conviction. I can't take it anymore. He says this every summer. Gets drunk and comes over to Ken's cabin, throws the door open in disgust. I mean it this time. His son wanders up and down the road, crying at night, huge sobs that keep us all up. He has just broken up with his girlfriend, his first love.

Sometimes the dogs get loose and don't come back or other dogs from other cabins escape to our place. Dogs rule the road; there are standoffs and yelping late in the night. We don't worry too much about it; they limp and wander home in time. The two men at the end of the road are strange and conversation turns tense when they show up at campfires. They are friendly enough and they work in the bush like everyone else but there's a twitch when they smile, slight like a blink. They have been known to flirt with other men's wives and girlfriends.

On the shore near the highway is an empty lot, cleared down to the water. From the centre of the lake you can see it, a space where nothing grows. Site of a residential school that stood for over thirty years. Massive building that was a forced home, a prison. Black spot where the building used to be. Still casts its shadow over the lake. Three young Indigenous boys died trying to escape the place, freezing on the lake on New Year's Day. They were trying to reach home—Nadleh, a little village at the east end of the lake. Tiny white steepled church, square houses on the knolls of the creek that flows both ways, full of salmon in the spring. Longing for home luring them in the dark and bitter cold.

Fraser Mountain rises up to the south with a large hump like a grizzly's in the middle. From the north side of the lake it is majestic but up close it is a pile of hills, some sheer cliffs. You can climb it or drive to the top, where there is a rickety lookout; metal stairs rise twenty metres up. Kids go there to party; there is spray paint all over the sides.

In the winter there is no one but us and the dogs and we reach close to the centre. Even in the middle of the lake on a boat, the world is not as clear and in its place. Underneath us the bottom is waiting to rise when the heat comes, maybe dismantle a few docks in the spring, slice off a bit more of the muddy shore. Small, disruptive changes, reminding us of its power.

Waning light brings us back, and hunger, the warmth of a fire by the truck. Ken and I have been coming to this lake all our lives; it is imprinted, part of our history. My family camped at the nearby site in a big canvas tent that leaked cold dew. Mornings, I drew pictures of flowers on it with a slow finger. Through the flap the sky like a mouth swallowed up the lake, let the birds shush through, the stars puncture.

Ormond Lake

Uncle Phil's Jeep is the cool kind, rugged and square, built for the backwoods, roads that aren't really roads but get broken in after a few tries. Dad sits beside him in the front; I'm nestled between Aunt Evelyn and Mom. We scramble for seat belts but Phil has already started down the steep driveway leading to the road along the lake. A storm has just passed, road swampy in places, leaves glistening. He looks over at us, blue eyes crinkling, boisterous laugh. It is late summer and a rancher lets his cattle herd graze all along the lake. They stand immovable as we drive up and watch us warily; they still don't move, even after their russet-and-white-splashed calves get scared and run into the deep ditches. Such big beautiful eyes. Uncle Phil gets impatient, honks and the giants slowly lumber off, annoyed at our interference.

We're off to see Ormond Lake, just north of Nadleh at the end of Fraser Lake. Reserve sits on rolling farmland, straddles a creek that flowed both ways until a huge dam was built upstream and changed its flow. Village fishers line the edge of the old bridge in the spring and fall; their lines glint like spun webs in the sunlight. They hardly look as we cross over. The kids do; they wave shyly and smile when we wave back.

We turn left on Dog Creek Road, which runs along the west side of the Nechako. You can't see it, I say, but it's just past the end of those fields, past an old farmstead still standing, a simple square home with small windows and sloping roof about to cave in. Our friend Eric, he was born there over eighty years ago, my mom says, and it's still standing. Old farmhouses hover like ghosts on the landscape everywhere around here. Farmers grab any good wood that they can salvage from the buildings and then leave them to rot. Because no one loves them, you can almost miss them, drive by countless times before you notice they're still there.

We turn left again on Sutherland Road, a logging road that goes up and behind the mountains that surround Fraser Lake. Lots of little lakes here, blue baubles on a string. Small fishing holes that are a treasure for fishermen looking for some peace. There's a fisherman that drives up here from California every year, my dad says. He grew up in Fraser Lake and loves that there is no one around. Even farther down the road, my mom says, there is a man who lives by himself in the bush; he can't read or write, gets work clearing roads in the winter, cuts wood for people—even saved a few hunters that have gotten lost.

My aunt adds her ringing laugh, pats my shoulder. We are the listeners, the messengers who bring the story back for the others, add a few lines of our own. How many logs get hauled out of here? my uncle asks over the din of the road. We pass whole chunks of raw land, shaved and torn, gravel spilling out of sides of hills like stuffing. Hard to get at some of these places, must have some expensive equipment, Uncle Phil says. He's a farmer, likes machines, how efficient they are at making money. Still harvests every year, even though he's retired. My aunt and mom are twittering in the back seat with me all snug between them, still feeling like the little girl who was excited when they came to visit.

Final left is to Ormond Lake, narrow wet road that leads to two small campsites and a boat launch. Across the lake is a lodge where Nadleh members go to heal, recover from addictions and illness. This lake is a traditional place to heal, I say, having read about it in a local newspaper. Lodge is new, rebuilt after years of disrepair. It sits on a little island in the middle of the lake, bright flags fluttering from poles in the ground, on the deck. Must have to canoe out there, I say as we get out and walk to the boat launch. Maybe crossing the water is part of the healing, starts before you even arrive. There is no one there that I can see. Lake is bigger than I thought; it looks like a coastal inlet, grey clouds shredding through the pines, remnants of a late afternoon storm. Puddles everywhere, strands of smoke coming from one of the campsites. Water is deep blue like the ocean, clouded from silt stirred from the storm. Bottom rising to the surface before is settles in some new spot.

All these hidden places, so amazing what comes up when you go down some roads. Places you never knew existed, my mom exclaims. She loves adventure, goaded my dad to leave the comfort of Manitoba before I was born to start a new life in BC. She goads him still: Let's go to Hungary, take a cruise on the Danube. She wants to see where her ancestors lived, the roads they walked on, breathe the air.

Just past the ring of spruce and pine around the lake, the surrounding hills are barren, charred remains of a forest fire that ripped through here last summer. Fire so intense that crews flew from California, Australia and Mexico to fight the flames. They stayed in long, beige tents, row on row along the side of the high-way. Like a barracks, getting ready for war. All down the Suther-land is a mess of mud, earth grey with ash, Dad says. Will take years for it to come back. Nadleh members fought to keep the flames from their sacred lake, their healing place. It came close— you can see withered stumps on the road in—but it passed by in the end.

We follow the smell of smoke, pungent in the moist air, to a huddle of roughed-out campsites: picnic tables, levelled gravel. A small camper snuggled in the best spot on the beach, shrouded in spruce boughs. A few kids run around the corner, followed by their mom, a sturdy Indigenous woman, who smiles at us briefly as we turn to leave. She's probably been coming here for years, knows all the best spots, Uncle Phil says. We pile back in the new Jeep; bare branches squeak along the sides as we pass, soft spruce needles we can hardly hear.

Stuart Lake

Friday afternoon, chocolate cake in our bellies and the cold wind whips, keeps the sun from melting, ice gripping the edges. Each day the tracks of sleds and skis surface like scars the lake has been holding, hidden by snow. Waiting for the spring to clear away traces, curves, spots where machines were stuck for hours. One year, a machine went through the ice, my colleagues tell me. This time of year when the ice is changing. High school sweethearts drowned; took days to find their bodies. Whole town turned out to search. The girl was from Nak'azdli. Her mother ran the clinic on reserve with such efficiency, no hint of disaster.

Six of us spread out in separate trucks pass the mouth of the Stuart River, taking chunks out of the ice, slow reclaiming after so much white. Wind chases us down Sowchea Road. Snow-drifts laced with gravel, the black outlines flow in crumbling swells against the hard hills to the south. We are in search of red willow, sturdy stems and branches cropping up along the edge of the road, ripe deep burgundy skin that makes strengthening tea, softens hair as you soak it. It's the season for them, the in-between time of slow spring. They stand out from the grey dead willows that will either rally or succumb to the earth.

I crank one of my favourite songs, "This Must Be the Place." It's by Talking Heads, I tell Marie. Do you remember it? I danced on my bed every afternoon to it until an annoyed nursing student down the hall pounded on my door. Everyone loves country music here, Marie had said, and she played drawl and twang at her desk until I told her I wanted to hang myself. So much sadness, I said, and she laughed, shook her long dark hair in waves and changed the channel.

We stop at a small bridge crossing a dark cold stream, assess the quality of snow. It is neither gumboot season nor winter boot season; hiking boots puncture holes or hold steady on the crust. We step gingerly, struggle up to our knees or skim, following moose tracks. Perfect nuggets of droppings mark the spot where the animal plowed through the stream to the other side.

We could swim here for our winter challenge, Laura says. It's calm, not too deep. I lean over the bridge, spot the clear bottom, smoothed by small currents. Edges are still ice, though, so we'll have to wait, I say. Don't want to be hauling ourselves armless like seals to the mucky shore. Sandy isn't here and she wants to come too, Marie says, ever thoughtful. I'll take the video; don't want anyone to see my pale stumps, Sarah says, and she smiles.

Soon the sun will do its job, break through the gloom to warm the water. Bridge is small, wood grey and rutted by studded tires, stark in the early spring. I look at the dark cold water flowing, think of Ophelia with her long hair spread, ringed with garden flowers, pink, orange, serene grass blades bending. Shocked look in her wide eyes just before she capsizes. I saw her likeness in an exhibition, an actress floating, holding the pose, but I was still shocked by the wholehearted giving in. She blinked in the picture like a watching animal, her thin wrists shuddered, next breath shallow through parted lips.

That will not be us. We'll run in like warriors, half-naked and yelling, attempt a full immersion and get the hell out, I say. Laura nods, says, We'll have to be quick. Dick's wife, she doesn't like us coming here, she'll come shoo us away like strays.

In Japan, I soaked in public baths and sacred mountain hot springs, constant sound of clear water running, surrounded by polite Japanese ladies who inquired about my tattoo: *What does that mean?* They pointed at the Arabic scrawl on the soft side of my wrist. Cleansing ritual accompanied by twitters of delight. *You are not married?* I would shake my head, no. *Good for you*, they would laugh, touch my bare shoulders soft like wings.

Laura calls for her dog Nessie as we stumble along the stream. She doesn't want her to get hit. People fly down these roads and she's so young, doesn't look. She's been hit already, has only a slight limp; lucky the vet knew what she was doing. Laura spent hours at her side. Nessie didn't learn how to cross the highway with the rest of the rez dogs; they're pretty smart, her husband says. He holds a tiny Pomeranian in the crook of his arm tender like it's a baby. Big voice, ball cap, beard and moustache combo that is common here. He builds roads, or drives the machines that make them, take chunks out of the sides of hills, move boulders like they are pebbles.

Marie uses wire cutters at the base of the willows, snaps them into a growing pile. I walk past her to a still spot by the creek, cold holding back the spring rush of water, but I can hear rustling in the branches nearby, whispers of birds, buds muscling in the taut bark.

Earlier, after the chocolate cake in the quaint work kitchen, Lee had said, You cannot live with the threat of a raised fist. Fear freezes, you forget to breathe and you can't wake up in the morning, forget to feed yourself, brush the hair out of your eyes. Out of nowhere she said that, throwing in chunks of pain in conversation, burning holes through words.

No room at the creek to skin the branches so we decide to head to Laura's place. Marie and I follow her, Lee and Sarah in the back; I can see their heads leaning in conversation. Laura takes the long way down muddy roads, patches of snow like clumped sugar. She stops, calls for Nessie and waits, patient as a stone, then gets back in.

After some futile circling on the myriad roads near the lake, we pull into a long driveway leading up to a log cabin with a long deck, barbecue, plush green couch and some chairs. Sun warms our backs and faces as we find places to settle. Laura's husband passes out cans of beer, offers puffs of a joint. Does your family have the cabin by the beach? Sarah asks, and I say, Yes but I've never been there. It's a giant slab of patched-up wood and added-on rooms that belonged to my uncle; my cousins use it now. No one looks after it but they love it, I say. Sounds like a lot of places around here, Laura says and sits on a step. Roads around the lake are a mix of expensive spreads and shacks, driveways cleared by snow blowers or narrow shovelled paths. It's the end of the line, that's what it looks like, Marie says, a breeze twisting her black hair. Nessie finally shows up and the Pomeranian snarls as she runs up to him.

Laura offers more beer and a joint. I have to drive, can't get too messed up, I say and Marie asks for a ride. We are warm and silly in the sun; I feel myself melt, my bones meld to the hard slats of wood. Lean back and let the light in, I say, soon it will be summer. Hard to believe but it's true, Lee laughs. We should get going on the branches, Sarah says and Marie divides them into piles and drops them at our feet. Laura passes out knives to slice off the bark. It is satisfying work, the long thin strands curling in my fingers, some smaller chunks in the hard-to-reach places. Exposed wood bare and white at first, fresh smell of green, then quickly brown from exposure to air and light. Look how fast they change, I say to Lee and she laughs like she's always known the inside of a tree.

Lower Road

Highway is hilly, winding, slick with snow. Slim shoulders on the way to Fort St. James, Mark says, so you have to be careful, cautioning like I am a six-year-old at the wheel. He is a confident driver and I am new to driving in winter conditions. February is gloomy. Light begins to lengthen, cold is bitter. I am weary of anticipating spring, some encouraging green and growth. During the week this narrow road is crammed with logging trucks, trees shorn of branches packed tightly, tied with black straps. My friend Diana was driving behind a sixteen-wheeler and a tree fell off, bounced in the road like rubber, stopped her dead. Lucky the gravel truck had been through so she didn't skid on the ice. She pulled off to the side, hazards flashing, swallowed back terror, had to pick up her kids at school. That such a sudden flash of disaster could strike, she said, and to slip by it.

We are going to a memorial, a celebration of life. I didn't know the young man but I know his mother, though not well. We sat together in the front row of the high school band, playing first flute. She was beautiful, popular, big brown eyes that drank in rivers of attention. Her son had been living in the Fort, as we called it growing up, working as a logger. One payday, he went to a party at a house on the reserve. A fight broke out in the basement, over money, maybe, drugs, some say, no one knows for sure. He was killed, beaten probably, and dismembered.

It's the first time I've been to the Fort in many decades. My brother played hockey here when he was young but I rarely went to the games at the freezing rink. Instead, I stayed home and played music, hung out with my friends. As we walk into Chief Kwah Hall, all the seats are taken; people from my hometown sit in the bleachers. I can see their faces, aging and sad since the last time I saw them in high school, so full of hope then. A choir of Nak'azdli singers sing hymns, simple, strong voices, no harmony. The spokeswoman, Marie, expresses the deep horror and sadness the community feels. The mother, still doe eyed and regal, stands up and honours her son's life, his bereft wife and young children by her side. Then other families come up and cry for their own missing children. Some have been gone for years. There are prayers and pictures of the lost. I have seen their round young faces on posters pasted on store windows, gas stations, the post office. Eyes glinting with life, smiles bursting or shy. There are probably people in the hall who know what happened that night, maybe even know what happened to the others.

At the end of the ceremony, Marie announces that everyone is welcome to go down to the house by the lake where the young man's remains were found. They will smudge the basement to heal his torn spirit, pray and sing. A stream of bowed heads as if on pilgrimage crosses the busy road through town and by an open-air hockey rink empty of players. Coffee steaming from mugs, toques askew on young heads. Men wear caps; women, subdued scarves. A sheer cliff watches over the frozen lake, blank stone eyes. Something deep in me resists. I do not want to see it, I say, and on our way home we stop at the grocery store. Pretty young girl with multicoloured hair is the cashier.

What did you do on the weekend? she asks. She is fresh faced, almost bald on the sides where her head is shaved. I live in Prince George, I reply, went out for dinner. I dig out my bank card. How about you? I was designated driver for some parties, she says. Where were the parties? I ask. Well, the ski hill was lame, she says. Everyone was out at Sowchea beach, or on the reserve. My cousin started crying for no reason at the bar. It was weird. She looks me in the eye. Booze will do that sometimes, a middle-aged woman says behind me, and the girl nods knowingly. She hands me my receipt and wishes me a great day.

A year and a half after the memorial I got a job with the Nak'azdli and moved to the Fort. My friends were shocked but I didn't hesitate. Years abroad had sloughed off any fears of change, so I took the chance to jump into a new place. I met Marie my first week, her soothing, calm energy the same in a conference room as it had been in Chief Kwah Hall. My job was to join the technical team to help the community understand the enormous changes happening to their land; natural gas pipelines were proposed, many of them, criss-crossing maps with sharp incisions. Armies of scientists and surveyors were mounting cameras in trees, spying on moose and bears, testing the water, drilling at water crossings, assessing various routes and rights-of-way. A picture of a wolverine, fierce and alone in a field, captured by a hidden lens showed up in a presentation. Pictures of wide swaths of barren earth slowly covering with grass after the disruption of burying a pipeline. It's another gold rush, I overheard in conversations, the dash and quick plunder, platitudes of assurance that everything would go back to normal, that everyone would get rich. Foreign markets hungry for the sweet gas sluiced from deep, deep down.

Our office was a former community care centre for children and the aged. Old cracked beige linoleum with brown borders and pink flowers, pink and beige walls, floral curtains and a full kitchen. Giant bathtub in the back room that used to soothe old bodies. We joke that we will turn the room into a spa but it slowly fills up with supplies, map tubes, leftover leaflets. The centre had become a neglected storage space for chairs, tables, disabled phones, broken-down sofas. We had to clear it out, whip it into shape, make a bustling office with new desks, names and titles printed on sheets of paper and taped to the doors and walls. Lengths of maps took up most of the spare space, full of dots and wavering red, green and blue lines.

One afternoon a young woman came into the office, asking for me. Are you an archeologist? Calm, measured voice, like she was reading lines from a book. I said no but she said, Follow me.

Walked out into the empty field next door. The grass has just been cut, she said, looking intently at the ground. I work in the office right there. She turned her head and gestured to a building beside my office. We translate books into Carrier, or the Dakelh language, she said. I saw the many heads bowed over their computers. When I stopped in to introduce myself, they rose up shocked like birds.

There's a bone in the grass, just over here, she said, leading me over to the edge of the field. Sweet smell of green in the air, tough bristles grazed my ankles. It was a sliver of bone, concentric rings edged in red and yellowish white, like the circles of a tree trunk. It's a human bone, she said, not a moose. I can tell the difference. What do you think? I leaned over, repeated that I wasn't an archeologist. It must be his, she said. She pointed across the field to the lake. The people from the party came across here that morning on their snowmobiles, black garbage bags full. We thought they had just butchered a moose. Didn't think anything of it; meat is butchered here all the time. They dug deep in the snow all over the territory, near the train tracks, by the river, to get to the earth so his body would not be brought together again.

Maybe you should call the RCMP, I said, chilled suddenly. Yeah, I will, she said. Silent nod and we both went back to our offices without introducing ourselves. When I left at the end of the day, I went to where the bone had been and it was gone.

Lower Road is a strip of gravel and dirt, just a few potholes running along the lip of Stuart Lake. Dusty in the summer, muddy in the fall and spring, glassy with ice in winter. Snow machines scream down the edge of the lake, plumes of snow flying. I can see the headlights in the dark from my front window, see them race beside me on my way to work. Speed limit of twenty kilometres per hour but no one bothers.

Houses on each side, some painted, some given over to the weather. A few old log cabins with lean-to porches at the back, small dark square windows etched in the bare sides. A few old cars haphazard in the yard, a wheelchair motionless on a front step. Bright yellow and red paint etches out the badge of Superman, bold lines jumping out from the side of a grey weathered shack. Some homes are cared for, toys in the yard for children to play with. Some are resolutely unloved. Log rounds gather at the doorways in the fall, waiting to be chopped; smoke huts crammed with fish haze the air. Homes stare straight down the sixty-kilometre length of the lake to where it curves out of view, somewhere about the forty-kilometre mark. From the shore you can just make out the shape of some islands, wild and moody like an inland sea. No one lives on them but they are used as campsites in the summer.

You know how to cut meat? a man calls to me from his yard, knife in hand. What do you have? I ask. Moose! We both laugh. I have never handled a weapon in my life. He carries on hacking, his wife by his side, smiling at me. Dogs chewing on the gristle and bones curl up contented in the yard.

In the morning the school bus barrels by and the driver beams and waves at me; teenage kids like bent reeds, nodding to the beats, blue buds in their ears, hardly look up. Some older men cut through an overgrown field to the highway, where the gas station sells hot coffee and bannock. Big yellow house next to the office has a large-screen TV glaring every morning in a dark living room.

When there is a death in the community, the body is brought to one of the homes on the reserve for a few days before the funeral; trucks line up outside on the rocky shoulders for the mourners to gather. There is food, coffee and tea, fires in backyards, a circle of singers and a guitar. Out of the blue, into the black, a lone voice starts and others slowly join in.

One end of Lower Road curves to join other roads on the reserve. The other connects to a paved road named after the estimable Chief Kwah, which bisects the reserve from the town, Nak'azdli on one side, Fort St. James on the other. Chief Kwah had four wives and many descendants still live on the reserve. Lower Road was part of his territory; he saw the sun rise and set from here, hauled in fish, planned the seasons. His wives and children lived together, inhabiting separate spaces.

There is a re-creation of the original fur trading post built on the shores of Stuart Lake, founded by Simon Fraser in 1806 but wrested away by the Hudson's Bay Company in 1821. There is the main trading post and some outbuildings that housed the workers and their families, a school, a store. Wood is dark brown and the windows are tiny. I imagine long winter evenings with no light. Sturdy boardwalks, a well-built dock and a small causeway, where boats would bring in supplies, where local people would dock with their furs from up the lake. Young girls hired for the summer flitting along in bright long dresses, frilled bonnets, long white gloves. Sturdy men in black with hammers, pounding horseshoes, staring into blazing fires.

The oldest church in the province is on the other side of the town, white paint and green trim, a tall thin steeple. Weddings still happen there, happiness refracted in the stained-glass windows. Floors creak and moan under the weight of history, of so many feet trampling in and out. Praying and hoping that God will look after them. Just past the church, on top of a rising hill, is the Nak'azdli cemetery, protected by a wire fence and an imposing gate. Some headstones, some fenced graves. Dried flowers, bright plastic ones in glass vases. Crosses like steadfast trees, offering comfort. One smooth stone stands out: Here lies Chief Kwah, who saved the life of Sir James Douglas.

James Douglas became the first governor of British Columbia, but before that he had his headquarters at Fort St. James, a gathering of weathered, drafty buildings huddled near the rushing Stuart River. I imagine him, weary and drained from the endless winter, resolved to enforce the law, dispel the violence that nicked at his conscience.

Two Nak'azdli men killed two of the Hudson's Bay Company's servants. In retaliation, the Company men killed one of the murderers; the other, named Noel, escaped for a few years but then one day he came back. The whole village was empty except for one woman who was expecting a baby any day, Laura tells me in the kitchen at our office, stirring soup for lunch. A passion for plants; she has chosen chickweed and devil's club to study this year, find out what they can heal.

Douglas found Noel and dragged him to the fort. The men beat him with garden hoes and sticks from campfires, she says, looking at me sideways. Noel traded really nice furs. Anyway, Douglas yelled at him about killing one of his men.

What happened when the Nak'azdli men came back from hunting? I ask.

Well, there was a huge commotion, you can imagine, and the whole village wanted to attack Douglas and his men but they went to Chief Kwah first and told him what happened. We hear rustlings from the office, scraping chairs and chatter heading our way. You stay here and stir the soup, Laura says, and I'll set the table. I take the wooden spoon from her, waft of salmon and corn thickening.

I can imagine Chief Kwah considering his foe as he walks with some of his men to the fort and knocks at the gate. Douglas, courteous but harried when he answers. Kwah observes Douglas's carefully cut hair, a curl twisting at the nape of his smooth, thick neck. While the two men talk about Noel, a knock is heard at the gate. Kwah says it's his brother, and with a creak and scrape, in rushes the whole Nak'azdli tribe, furious eyes, cursing and flashing their knives.

Douglas's men are outnumbered, scrambling for defence. Douglas raises his gun to shoot but then the Chief grips both his hands in a firm fist. A long hard stare between them. Kwah's grip dry and unrelenting. Your hands are like chicken bones, he says. I could break them, roast them on this fire. I could break you. Douglas does not answer, his wife screaming, held back by the swarm. All around them the slash and scrape of knives.

The Chief's warriors swing their weapons over Douglas's head, taunting him, grazing his ear, becoming bold.

Shall we strike? Shall we strike?

Louise, the daughter of an old trader and an astute interpreter, cries out, You! to a respected Chief she knows. Do not let this happen or it will never end!

She throws a blanket and tobacco into the crowd, rushing to grab more things. The other women rain clothes, pipes and utensils on the heads of the warriors from the rafters, all the while begging them to spare Douglas's life. It reminds Kwah of voices singing hymns at church. A smile starts slow at the edges of his lips; his grip loosens, fingers slide to his sides. Released, Douglas leans on a table. A man comes to Kwah and they speak quietly until Kwah raises his right hand to his chest, signifying his acceptance of the gifts as a compensation for Noel's death. Seeing the decision made, the Nak'azdli tribe gathers the goods and slips into the night.

December morning, roads iced, sky sharp blue cut with bulbous clouds. Melissa, Ronnie and I are driving to the airport. Back seat is stuffed with clothes and toys, Melissa's two-year-old son's domain. Radio blaring country, which I complain about so she changes the station. How can you not like country? she asks. You're from here. She looks at me in her mirror, big brown incredulous eyes. I smile.

This is much better. I lean my head back, let the weak winter sun warm my face. I sing with the Waterboys; Melissa and Ronnie chat, snickering at me.

We pass through town, a series of small strip malls, dollar stores, banks, the post office, Subway, the grocery store. Blank stare of boarded windows like knocked-out teeth. Copper mine just started up outside of town but there is no spillover of wealth that I can see. Everyone talks about how the town has been passed over. Only change is a series of swank townhouses close to the lake for company workers to stay in. Outside the credit union a ring of Nak'azdli members, old and young and in between, gather to chat, sometimes to pass a swig of a bottle. They spread out on the sidewalk in a loose line like they are waiting for a parade, and they let people pass, chatting with the ones they know. There is laughter, friendly jostling, some scowling. Sometimes the RCMP drive up and talk to them for a while and then they get back in their trucks.

There is one liquor store in town and the cashiers are savvy women, joshing with the customers, looking everyone square in the face, smiling. That debit machine is as slow as a turtle walking backwards, a cashier with bouncy dark hair levelled with me one time. And keep the card in there, she said. It's the men, I've noticed, that keep taking it out and putting it back in. We all had a laugh. She knows everyone, what they drink, calls them out if they switch it up, is patient with customers counting out change in shaking hands. You're cut off, I heard her say to a teenage girl trying to buy a mickey of vodka. It was noon on a Saturday. I saw you trying to walk and it wasn't pretty.

Where is the turnoff again? Melissa slows down and Ronnie points to the next left. We follow a few tire marks, drifts deeper here. Small wood house, sharp square windows with no paint, bare sheath like blotchy skin. Just past it a big green building emerges in a cleared field. That must be it, I say. We pull in by a white crew cab, the rig of choice in the north, and I get out just as Barry, the pipeline router, emerges with a steaming coffee in his hand. We're just warming up, he says. Be about ten minutes. He is middle-aged, gruff, serious about his work, anxious that he may have to amend the snaking line he's traced for the pipeline to follow. Ronnie's trapline will be passed through. She is here to see what may be cut, how close to memories as essential as skin.

The helicopter pilot walks up to us, blades whirring behind him. Smoking a cigarillo, he chats with us, strong French accent. Have you been in a helicopter before? Melissa and Ronnie are sharing a cigarette, circling us with smoke and coffee steam. None of us have. Pilot raises an eyebrow in surprise. So I must tell you a few things, he says. Do any of you get carsick? We look at him blankly. It hadn't occurred to me, accustomed to the relative smoothness of planes, that the ride would be rocky. If you look at the map a lot you may get woozy, so just look at the horizon so you'll know where you're at, the pilot says. There are sick bags but you must let me know if you are going to be sick. Slight look of amusement passes through his eyes.

We walk out to the helicopter in a careful line, settle in our seats, adjust headphones and find the button to push if we want to talk. It is like sitting in a very loud metal bowl. We rise straight up, waver a little and shift north, over the village, snow-covered homes, blank white yards, strings of muddy roads. The thin steeple and outline of the church by the lake looks like a plastic pawn in a chess game. In a war, it would be a target.

We will follow the line all the way up to Nation River, an hour from town, to cover the proposed pipeline route and the suggested alternatives. Pilot radios in the plan and coordinates to ground control, who repeats back in a sleepy voice: Two and a half hours' fuel and five souls on board.

Land stretches out pockmarked with deep half-frozen lakes, rocky outcrops, jagged lumps. Sides of sloping hills shorn; every day semi-trailers roll grimy through the main road, stacked with logs stripped of branches, fresh pulp smell undercut with grease. Flying in closer to the line, the land is ripped up by recent make-shift logging roads that may become highways the pipeline will follow. So much disruption. I see the concern on Ronnie's face.

There's a moose! Melissa says, but I miss it. Barry points out a hunting cabin close to the line, small and perfect, out of a winter postcard. We'll route away from there, he yells into his mouthpiece, and we shift again, my stomach lurching, to follow the steep banks of a lake. Farther north, the line edges the mine, a large expanse of flat grey land, neat rows of buildings, no massive trucks or machinery that I can see. It looks silent, unpeopled, all the workings and movement happening in the ground in noisy hangars—the mess of taking out a mountain just out of our sight.

We're too close to the river here, Barry says. He points out an alternate route and Ronnie nods silently. Mountains start to join forces at the Nation River, ground gathering up instead of spreading. More crowding trees but they would soon be gone too; we follow the side of a mountain, cross a steep ravine and a logging road slung to the side, rough and rocky.

On the way back we follow the road and the pilot chats with Barry about the winner of a lottery who gave away his fortune to charity that morning. Don't know if I'd do that, he chuckles. I keep my eyes on the horizon so I know where I'm at. We pass through little troughs of snow and then blinding spots of sun, bouts of wind batter and then we are clear again. We pass over untold stories, sacred areas, bears huddled in sleep.

We take pictures of ourselves, bright smiling faces, views of trees, rocks, lakes in the background. Our first trip a success, though I see traces of sadness in Ronnie's face as we settle back in the car.

Sharp, clear day in late October, we climb Mount Pope, imposing steep crag that watches over the lake. It happens every year in the town; some run, some walk and some parents drag their dawdling, complaining kids. Steep rocky sections followed by undulating paths through spruce and pine, smell of musky fall pleasant at the back of my throat. I walk with Alice, sixty-seven and sprightly, curious, full of stories of life and travel. She was a respected teacher in the town for a long time. Famous for her healthy cooking, her chalet-style home perched on a bluff overlooking the lake.

Mountains are holy in Japan, I tell her in the level spots. Pilgrims drink clear, cold water on the way, clap three times to let the mountain gods know they're coming. Runners in bright gear, earbuds, speed past as we stop for water, talk and climb and rest. Alice tells me how she and her husband met the land where her house is, how they spent hours on it, just feeling it. It felt good; it was the land we wanted, she says. We'd built another house in town but it didn't feel like home. We took our time with this place, let the land speak to us before we decided where to put the house. Each time we sat in a different place, deciding where the rooms would be, the best vista for taking in the lake. And the land speaks to us still; it is a happy place, everyone feels it when they come to visit.

We started at nine in the brisk fall morning and by eleven we have stripped our jackets, dug out our sunglasses. Last year the whole mountain was covered with snow, she says. Winter comes early to the tops of mountains, hangs on long into the spring. We start a grind of switchbacks, steep with breathless sweat, and then a reprieve of five minutes of flat, then the switchbacks again. We're getting close, she says, but then around the next bend the vista she was expecting does not appear. So we keep going. Bitter wind picks up on the bare spots. Stuart Lake stretches around the mountain like a moat, dotted with islands where the Nak'azdli painted and etched pictures of animals and weapons on rugged stones, ancient story of life.

Smell of smoke and crackling—two sturdy women in winter coats and headbands offer hot chocolate and M&M cookies. Started out on the trail at six this morning; it was still dark, had my headlamp on the whole way, the blond one tells us, steaming cups in her hands. I am grateful for rest; the final steep stretch is just ahead. Young kids are tramping the bushes, coming out with sticks and fencing with each other, their parents engrossed in conversation. A tall man with a ruddy face and red hair flapping runs by. Alice tells me he drives twenty hours from Alberta every year to run up the mountain and back, that he searches the internet for community runs to attend.

Warmed and nourished, we start the final ascent. The wind rips harsh so we have to lean in to the rocky face, use our hands to crawl in places. A white gazebo marks the top of the summit.

A young man in a blue windbreaker takes our picture; we are both beaming and windswept, the hills around us grey with dead pine mixed with spiky thin spruce. The Stuart long and winding around a curve, smaller lakes off to the east, strips of sand edging, looking cold, braced for winter. Already the fish are hiding at the bottom, slick scales hidden in the weeds.

I receive a message from my colleague that there will be arrests made regarding the murder of the young man, almost two years later. Three out of the four are from Nak'azdli. There will be a strong reaction in the community, she warns, but what I hear mainly is that people started talking; the burden of fear had silenced them for so long. Marie talked of hosting another event so that the community could speak and grieve and start the process of healing. It may happen yet. As it is such a small community, everyone is connected in some way, through relations close or distant, to those who were arrested. On the radio one morning, the father of the young man spoke of the intense relief he felt following the arrests with its hope of closure, and he spoke of the unrelenting pain of the loss that he and his family endure.

By this time, I have been driving back and forth on Lower Road for four months, home for lunch, check the mail, run errands. Many mornings I park in front of the office and walk across the road to an empty field and take pictures of the blossoming day, haze of the moon floating on a pink-blue sky. Stuart Lake is an inland sea, with all its moods, sudden, sometimes violent changes. In the morning the clouds ball up in the centre, its own weather created overnight, hovering, holding history, all the racked bent backs and hands raised in joy.

Often I am joined by Laura, who has expanded her interest in plants to gather roots, berries and leaves from the land to make medicines, some of which she sells in little round pots and zip-lock bags. Sarah follows, a trained teacher who asks astute questions of presenters, stumping them into silence. We gather by the lake to marvel, taking pictures that cannot capture the combination of rugged rocks, fading moon, changing light.

I remember the day the young woman pointed in the direction of the house in which the young man was found but I didn't want to look. I knew it was on Lower Road and I took furtive glances here and there. And then one day, a bright early fall morning, I saw the house, which had been demolished after it had been smudged that February morning; an empty lot of tall green grass to one side, a small house with light yellow siding on the other. Maybe the beauty of the morning emboldened me. A pile of wrecked timber, plaster, bits of plastic, seasons weathering the rough edges, yellow insulation soaked and shredding, boards jagged and pointing. Two freezers and a washing machine on a small platform, hauled out of the house but never taken away.

Red Car

Driving east down Highway 16, the Highway of Tears. Clear December morning, road twinkling in the low sun, diffuse like tea water. Sky like a dome, lid letting light in cracks. Listening to the CBC mumble of voices. I watch a red car pull up to a slow stop on a country road, cross the highway into another road.

When I pass the mouth of dirt, the red car is waiting for me; somehow it has turned around while my eyes drifted. It pulls onto the highway, deliberate, a careful aim. Bull's eye to the side of my car. I can see a bald head, hands on the wheel. Round eyes, I imagine them black. Ghoul in the red car scrapes the side of my car, keeps driving into me, not fast, not stopping. Casual, like a snowplow clearing a path.

Still going highway speed, I veer over the centre line as he scrapes into me. And I keep going like nothing happened. But then I stop because I can no longer hear the radio mumble, just my breath. On the shoulder a few hundred metres later, my feet light on the gravel, I walk around to the bruised side. Red streaks like candy-apple nail polish. I look up to the red glow of the red car tail lights, gleam of headlights as they flash across the highway, waiting for me on the country road.

Bald ghoul in the car. No reflection of his black eyes in the mirror, no glint of a face in the side mirror. But I feel it taking me in. I stand on the shoulder, see the breath steam from my mouth, feel the eventual steady beat of my heart. He does not get out. He does not move.

I am both standing and swirling. When I was nineteen I was in a car that spun out of control and my eyes fixated on my hand on the dashboard. Like I could hold the car in one place and there was such peace in the centre of that chaos. Like I could control the outcome, or I had surrendered. When the car stopped spinning, my hand was still on the dashboard, holding things together. Front end bashed into a telephone pole.

Two country roads that meet at the highway, red car scuttling across. Turning around, scuttling across again. Small and shiny in the dawn light like a scarab. I can never remember exactly which roads but I remember the view. Mumbling on the radio. Late for my class, I was stepping on it. If I am alone, I slow down and read the road names. McCauley. Stump. Snell.

4

Williston Lake
Kemess Lake

Williston Lake

Young pilots double as baggage carriers, cramming every space on the plane with boxes of food, suitcases, strollers, packages of medicine. We strap in, twelve of us; some are going to Kwadacha, just north of Tsay Keh Dene. Twin engines climb. Flat land of the interior, contours hidden by snow skiffs, breaks into frozen waves, like a pod of whales emerging from the earth, pushing up. Little plane swerves down narrow ravines, snow wrecking the view, blasts of cool shuddering the thin wings. A black river squiggles, squished between chunks of steep grey granite.

Trucks line up like sentries to pick up the loads, people stuffed in cracks, draped over boxes. Irene and I squeeze in the back seat of Nick's truck. He drove up yesterday, carrying enough food to feed the village for two dinners, a lunch and a breakfast; took him seven hours on active logging roads. Nearly got run off a few times, he says, crinkled, serious eyes. He has worked for Tsay Keh for ten years.

Town is a ten-minute drive on a white-caked rolling road. Signalled by a squeal of snowmobiles and then the sight of them racing down gravelly streets. More sleds than trucks in this town, Irene says. It is dusk and light beams from the machines waver into the thin black trees. Irene gestures to the white sheen of a mountain hovering. Looks like a smushed-up pyramid, she says. Watches over us like a pharaoh with a crooked nose.

Irene is an Elder in training. She was born in Finlay Forks, a village erased by the Bennett Dam. Graveyard with all our ancestors was flooded, she tells me, bones washed out and mingled with all the dead animals. We moved a few times and Tsay Keh is where we live now but it isn't home. Irene is short and voluble, given to giggles and sudden angry rants. On the flight out, she held her book an inch from her eyes, searching out the words as if learning a secret code. When I met her outside a casino years later, she didn't recognize me at first. Only after she slid her glasses down her nose did she home in.

One building for the school and band office makes up the hub of the town. Cop shop, store, teacher's residence stolid in the snow. A new training centre being built with industry money, designed with big windows to take in all the light. We stay in the residence, a long flat-roofed building, with six rooms, two bathrooms, a kitchen. Beds are single, two to a room, linoleum floor with beige and brown squares like a hospital. Houses and small cabins huddle on streets named in the Sekani language: *sas*, bear, I recognized. Irene taught me *khuda*, moose; *tsa*, beaver. Windows small and black, a few kids walking to the store, dogs racing ahead. Yards of gravel. Hard to grow things up here, Irene says. Soil is thin and then it blows away.

Irene and I walk out to the reservoir before dinner, 250 kilometres long, stroke of a pen in an engineer's office. Williston Reservoir a lumpy carpet, swollen stumps poking the surface. Wide valley, wall of white mountains creates a chute for fierce winds. They didn't clear anything, Irene says, they just dammed the Peace and let the water flow. Killed all kinds of animals. We saved some moose, paddled out and hauled them back to shore. Nights we heard them struggling in the water, calling to each other. Wind is sharp, disc of January sun setting. Tsay Keh flag ripples, like an outpost on a distant planet.

We have pancakes and sausages in the school gym the next morning. Long lineup of teachers, cops, band office workers, Elders at the front with metal canes. Tables with white paper covers, paper plates. A thin young man with long dark hair walks in, ethereal, blue-grey vacant eyes. In a dress, he could've been Ophelia; I can picture flowers wreathing his small skull. He drank antifreeze a few years ago, hasn't been the same, Irene tells me. He laughs with the children, drifts by the food and hovers in a corner.

Some of the men have a wild look, stomping in oversized boots, muscles taut or bellies jiggling over. Ladies who teach Sekani move their bodies gingerly, shuffling in slippers, settling into seats as if lowering into scalding water. Their dark heads lean into each other as they eat, as if straining to hear a soft tune. Faces weary until a smile breaks through, then passes.

Irene and I join the two Elder men, Francis and Martin. They nod to me and eat in silence, go up for seconds, wrap plates in plastic. They are widowers, feed themselves as well as they can, chop wood for the widows, light their morning fires. Irene tells them we will come by for interviews in her laughing way. Don't clean up just because we're coming, she hoots. Basketballs pound the gym floor, kids squealing; a loose game starts but the meal is over and everyone drifts out, no bell to remind them.

We drop by Martin's place, a small two-room cabin with a blazing stove. Martin is my husband, Irene tells me at his door. I left him years ago. He asks me to come back, but I can't live here anymore. Door opens to a wall of heat; he picks clothes off the couch. Laundry is strung in shreds across the ceiling. One lamp on the table, room shapeless and dark around him. Glasses low on his nose, he looks confused as his rough fingers trace the map we lay out. It is too dark to read, I can't mark any spots, he says, his voice gravelly and plaintive, looking at Irene. He gestures to the window behind us.

That big mountain that watches over Tsay Keh is Deserters Mountain. Named after some gold miners who left some young boys behind when they ran out of food. They were heading north to the Klondike. Gold rush made people crazy. Deserters Mountain with the crooked cap, Irene says, packed white with snow except for the tip, chipped like a jagged arrowhead. It turns pink and purple at sundown, Irene tells me, casts a ghost shadow across the town.

There is a meeting in the gym that night. A man from Vancouver is reading through a new election code, his bald head bowed to papers, an executioner reading the list of those doomed. Jeers from a skinny lady whose house has no insulation. There is mould in the walls; my children are sick, she cries out. Her son, equally skinny, stands with her. They sway and raise their fists. I appreciate your problem but I have to keep going, the man says. He keeps going. The lady and her son stand up again, repeat their story, louder. A little girl wanders from her mother to stand and gaze at the crowd. A former Chief stands up, gives a speech about the deplorable living conditions, how builders come with cheap materials and make shoddy houses. It's because we're Indians and they don't care, he says. The man stops, waits for the Chief to finish, keeps going. Now we have to vote on the new election code, he says. He stands up, a short, stocky man, stubborn face, crossed arms.

From an open door I can see Deserters leaning in, blocking the late afternoon light. Raise your hands to pass the election code, the man calls out. Stands there like a boxer waiting for the match decision. Not much happens, then a few arms are raised, then a few more. Enough to pass. People gradually stand and the chairs are moved to make way for dinner tables. Kids bundle up to play in the bright afternoon; dogs stand at the doorway, lured by smells of ham and potatoes.

That night there is a gathering in the living room of the residence. Coffee is poured and we all sit on two brown leather couches with no springs left. Your butt touches the floor in these things, I tell Irene. They've been here forever, she says. An old Chief, Irene's brother, defiant long black hair, tells the story of how Francis joined their family: Francis was ten years old and his parents were killed in a car accident on the way to Prince George. He was used to being on his own, his parents taught him the old ways, so it was a while before he realized they weren't coming back. He set his traps for foxes, groundhogs, wolverines. Animals talked to him as he set them, kept him company. He chopped and brought wood in and waited until my father came down the road to his cabin and said, You're coming with me.

Costco cookies and dried elk meat are passed around, TV with the hockey game blaring in the corner. Little girls with round open faces listen and look at me until they are carried away crying for school the next day. After the peals of snowmobiles ease off and Deserters Mountain is swallowed by black, the coyotes run through the village, mournful yips like crying babies.

Irene and I go to Francis's place the next day. We are in Tsay Keh to interview Elders for a traditional use study, learn how they used the land, stories the map lines tell. House a yellow box, sleds pulled up on the front yard, brown mutt tied up, barking. A small man, he stands in the curtainless window, watching us gather our maps, notebooks. Another man answers the door, dark eyes jumpy, searching our faces. Francis quiet behind him. This is Evan, he says, my son, as we step inside his kitchen. Evan smiles, strokes a nervous hand through his black hair, strands of kinky white. Plaid shirt half done up, ski pants and bare feet. Hole in one of the kitchen walls, some male voices in the basement.

Irene and I lay out maps on the kitchen table, my hands shaking as I tack them down. Eyes watching me. We're here to do some interviews, Uncle Francis, find out what you know about the land, mark it down, Irene says. Evan is behind us; something fidgeting inside him. Francis silent, arms at his sides. Deep-set, heavy-lidded eyes, white wisps of hair scattered across his pale head. He steps closer to the maps, peering at them as if over the edge of a cliff. Need my glasses, I'll go get them, he says and moves off to the living room, lifts blankets until he finds them.

Evan leans in, smells of sweat, oil, smoke. Rough finger traces folds, ridges, blue waterways. Voices from the basement grow louder, come pounding up the stairs. Two stocky boys, T-shirts, track pants and bare feet, stand in the kitchen. Evan calls to them, says, These are my brothers. Two men Evan's age follow, faces closed, edge in and pour some coffee. Sun spills in, makes a pale square on the map. Hard to see, Evan says, but there are no curtains to pull. Francis comes back in, glasses in hand.

We want to know where the cabin is, Irene says to Francis, the one where you were born, where my daddy found you. It was on a lake, Francis says, voice froggy from disuse. He hovers closer, asks where Ten Mile is. Evan and Irene consult and point it out to Francis. The men stand and listen, smell like Evan plus something else. They smell my fear, see my unsteady hands.

Francis studies the map, confusion drifting in and out of his cloudy eyes, listens and doesn't listen to Evan, to Irene. Glasses on and off his face, a broad hand across his skull, smoothing the hairs. Picture of him and his wife, now dead, framed and mounted on a wall behind him. He jabs a finger at a small lake huddled in high ridges. That's quite a ways from town, Irene says. Are you sure? Yes, Francis says and retreats to the living room and sits heavily, arms above his head as if in surrender.

With his declaration the men in the kitchen put on boots to head outside. Relief sweeps through me like a cold wave: they are gone. Machine whine of a snowmobile and Evan shucks on his boots to join them. When we go to say goodbye, Francis's arms are crossed and his head has nodded to his chest. You can see the whole of Deserters Mountain from your front window, Irene says as we leave. Blank wall of mountain hiding the last bit of sun.

We do the rest of the interviews at a small log cabin, plank wood tables, black-and-white pictures in stacks on the floor. Some in frames, nailed high up on the walls. Burble of the coffee maker in the background, pot of Labrador tea on the stove. An Elder comes in and the maps confuse her. Not used to looking at the land like this; I don't know where I am, she says, her eyes deep in her round face, greying hair in a tight bun. But Irene shows her where Tsay Keh is, a little dot at the top of the wide reservoir, the road to Kwadacha, the white folds of mountains like craters, and her finger follows her memory down paths that we track with bright stickers, sharp pens.

Last interview and we trudge back to the residence. Martin's truck is running; he's chatting with the old Tsay Keh Chief outside. You should spend some time with Martin, the Chief says. He knows everything about this place. He can drive you up to Ten Mile Lake, it's not far from here. Irene has already slipped inside the residence, and I'm caught. I haul myself up and buckle in. Cab is as hot as his cabin, my face is blazing. He rolls slowly on the gravel road out of town. My hand grips the door handle, rising panic.

Skinny pine trees crowd the side of the road, sky streaked with grey, clouds sweeping in with the start of snow. Truck picks up speed. Just over there I saw a UFO land; it came down black and fast out of the sky, Martin says, pointing to the left. Ingenika River flows through a valley just over there. My body goes cold, rigid, as the road climbs and sways. His breath streaks the window.

I went to town and got Alex, my son, to come with me, and we drove down a spur as far as we could, Martin says. Got out and tromped through the snow on foot. Day like today, but we couldn't find it. No sign, nothing. He looks for a response and I nod, my hand still on the door handle.

Some Elders talked about UFOs and large beings they had seen out in the mountains. Huge, hairy, fast-moving men that climbed cliffsides in minutes, threw boulders at them in tight traverses. Round black stickers were used for supernatural places, a whole valley spotted with them. They spoke with stricken faces, wonder in their voices. Dark starts to close in, white of steep snowbanks glows pink in the last light. Road ribbons through deep gullies and comes to a turnoff. To the right there are no tracks, no tree fringe. Raw path to the lake. Martin turns to me and says, I'm not going to do anything to you. He eyes my hand on the door handle. I take a breath and let go.

Kemess Lake

Johnny says he can see the plane coming, dark cipher in the blustery sky that curves. Pivots to point at us, standing in a line: a jumble of six bodies, our luggage strewn in colourful clumps. Clear cold autumn, bracing for snow. Pilot steps out from the small hole of a door, wind flapping his hair straight up dirty blond, eyes us before he talks, expert once-over. Shakes our hands, says emergency exits are at the end and the side of the plane, pull the lever and jump. No bear spray in the plane, please, cans explode if there's too much pressure. There's food and water for nine days if anything happens. Round, ruddy face, toothy grin of an eager boy. Logged twenty-nine thousand kilometres, short version of CV in clipped phrases, knows the narrow valleys behind the rolling sweeps, secret land hiding outside the moat of plateau. Edges of bare mountains, lonely for trees, some green.

Earmuffs are nestled in our seats, giant ones that hug your head. I suggest you wear those, he says as we squeeze and bend down the aisle. Things could get loud. When we take off, engine drones between two notes, one just higher than the other, sound reverberates, rattles through us, combustion hymn accompanies slight dips of wings. We were supposed to have left yesterday but a storm socked in; a six-hour window will get us there, another cold front coming in. Maureen, a researcher like me, raring to go like a first-grade teacher, sits beside the pilot in the cockpit; she flew with her ex-husband years ago, can read maps in an instant, watches the hovering dials.

Maureen's helping up there, maybe we won't die, Diana laughs. She has been on many flights, helicopter drops on mountaintops. Archeology digs and finds in crevices, fields of deep beauty she doesn't speak much of, keeps going back for more.

Says she needs it, misses the rugged ground working her body, revealing only what she can find on a given day.

Leaning over the narrow aisle, Johnny tells me he made $270,000 at the mines in one year; spent it on his grandchildren, bought them clothes, games. They swarm his house when he comes back, buzzing with desires, urgent needs. One granddaughter got $9,000 braces. He won $20,000 in bingo one night and got into a fight with his wife. Gives away his money and goes back for more. When we get to the mine, men in grey torn sweaters and plaid padded shirts will come up and shake his hand. Best tree faller in the province, they will say, wiry and fearless. Lined face lean, weathered like outdoor men around here. Looks at me sideways when he talks; thin lips cave to the hollow of no teeth, making his speech fuzzy. Eyes direct, knowing, but he's not telling. Sometimes he goes to the casino, he told me on the tarmac, lighting a smoke behind a roughened hand. He is gristled sinew, slips through the woods. Sixty-seven and bound by boots that will withstand anything, steel-toed, waterproof up to his knees. Was in a truck that went off the edge, broke three ribs. No gentle slopes where we're going, he says, only steep drops; you need vigilance to stay clear.

We lean west, toward Smithers, Rockies bluish in the sharp east light. Land rolls out in autumn, glowing, subtle. Diana takes out her camera, homes in on the changing views, snaps when she catches something. The light, the way it clears or crowds a place, that's what I'm after, she tells me. There's Fort St. James, she points out between takes. Mill town on the lip of lapping Stuart Lake. Long rough history of pioneers built into the narrow streets, pounded ground, spikes of railway, a cluster of houses. Vanderhoof is off to the left; can't see it on this pass. It's where the pilot lives, takes off on the nodding Nechako; it's where I grew up, three-storey house on a quiet street. I walk by it sometimes to check on the lilacs; thick bramble we could see out the living room window, bloomed light and pungent each May. Town criss-crossed in the shallow valley, hammered up quickly, efficient, graceless buildings, pushed at the pace of industry. At night the train from Prince Rupert rumbled our house, a ship on solid sea. Lonely whistle cool piercing edge of sleep. It struck me deep, tuning fork humming first note of going. We pass long, deep Babine Lake, just a few homes on the edge that I can see. An hour from Prince George and the runs on Hudson Bay Mountain are carved as if by scalpel, such bare precision. Houses tucked into neat valleys, roofs and walls blending with the ochre leaves, yellow grass, lean into humped hills. Dots of horses, cows, ranging farmland. Looks like a toy town, all smooth and clean, before the cowboys come and rough it up.

Black line of airstrip rises up in a field next to the golf course and we touch down. Pilot plays there sometimes, needs to work on his swing, he says, clutches a shoulder, grimaces. We trundle out, Johnny leading, then Irene, hunched in her raincoat, broad-cheeked smile. She read the whole way, a book she leaned into with intensity, shifting her eyes above her glasses for a better view. Followed by Diana and Jaclyn, both lean, tomboyish, long blond hair, though Diana's frames a serious face, Jaclyn's smooth, clear with youth. Maureen bustles ahead with the pilot, straight greying hair flapping in the wind, face lined with smiles. We're in for a quick nip to the washroom and a coffee for the road. Pilot says that he'll follow the valleys to the mine site; he can't get above the cloud cover, wants to see the peaks so he can clear them. Should take about an hour if the weather holds. We gravitate to a glass case in the middle of the small airport, a stuffed grizzly caught mid-stride. Small, glazed eyes guiding such an enormous body.

Rich is at the airport, playing games on his phone, greets us with an easy smile, matching stride. An anthropologist, effusive words that slip through his hands, enthusiastic waves. Got any bear spray? pilot asks, and Rich digs for it, adds his pack to the pile. We click back in our seats, rest our ears in the enormous protectors and in ten minutes leave the safety of the valley. Half-hour more and we leave autumn's still beauty for granite peaks, rising, enclosing. Engine blots out efforts at chatter. Plane circles down, valleys narrow to make room for squiggly rivers, lake shaped like a small *h*, I can see the hump. Shrubs instead of trees on mountainsides, then gravel, then grey rock rimmed with dull snow; barefaced when they pop out of the clouds.

Feels crammed in, I say to Irene. Think we're lost, she says, looks concerned. She came here as a girl with her family, old trails rubbed into the earth. She's been here on planes like this, bigger ones, hovering helicopters; an Elder surveying the land. Eyes of industry do the guiding. They wear hard hats and stand on gravel and shale-topped humps in the wind; they show her where the gold is, what mountain will be sacrificed.

How do you know? I say. She gestures impatiently to the pilot, to Maureen, maps flapping, hiding the shallow window. We circle down again, follow another raw valley, scraped earth comes closer and Irene's face relaxes. I think we are near it now, she says, slight smile.

Mine site is a clump of beige buildings, dirt edged, blends in with the racket of gravel trucks so huge I can see them before the runway levels, brown and smoothed, hemmed in by rough mountains. Stumble off and two men in plaid shirts, weary anxious eyes, throw their packs on the ground, ready to go. Plane didn't make it in yesterday. Behind them, a grimy school bus with the back door open; we lift our packs to waiting hands. When we climb on, Barney introduces himself, small, grey like the hills, torn plaid jacket, gentle smile. He flips the door closed and rumbles the bus off the strip. Mountains look mined already, tired, bleak; next in line to be shorn, stripped and gutted, crunchy insides sorted on grates by grimy hands.

There's the shop, supply room, Barney says, beckoning to bland buildings. We strain to see out the grubby windows, fall light showing the grim shapes. Utilitarian outlines of what is required. Here is the recreation room, the kitchen, the dormitories where you'll sleep. He drops us off in the mud in front of the dining room.

Cutting 'er close, he says, coming this time of year. Was snowing here this morning, turned to freezing rain.

Gruff-voiced woman, all business at the office, gives us our keys. Girls on the main floor, guys one up. We straggle up the wooden planks to our building, drop our bags in our rooms. Crank the baseboard heat, sound taps through all the open doors. On the wall above my single bed, written in precise black marker:

I dip't my oars into the silent Lake,
And, as I rose upon the stroke, my Boat
Went heaving through the water, like a Swan;
When from behind that craggy Steep, till then
The bound of the horizon, a huge Cliff
As if with voluntary power instinct,
Uprear'd its head.

Surprise stops me, not that the walls are a scroll, a space taken up with bored musings, but what is *this* doing here? Maureen pokes her head in, reads it with a laugh. Some miners read lots, want to leave their mark. I read it in school, she says, Wordsworth, all about how nature is so much bigger than you. Rooms are like the hostels in Asia, I tell her. Compact, bare, but with a single fan whirring. Dropping my bags, I bounded out to the streets, only noticed the chipped beige walls in the parched morning, Thai ladies rasping laughs, gossip out the window. Rooms unloved like this. There are washers and dryers next to the showers, a woman in the hallway says. Soft folds of flesh beneath loose T-shirt, track pants; wry smile shows a few teeth missing.

We head back to the main hall for food and the office lady calls out, You guys had your safety training yet? I'm starving but there is only time for snacks. We stock up on cookies, freshly washed grapes in baggies. Five courses for dinner, written on a chalk board. *Chicken pot pie* makes my stomach rumble. Kitchen is stocked, spotless. Cook calls out to us, lone voice hidden in the shiny machinery, anxious, with an edge that runs through it, thin blade. Where you from? What are you doing here? Light bounces off his glasses, round spot on his forehead. Obedient machines hum and rumble, slow combustion. Rich stops for a quick chat but we have to hustle back out to the bus where Barney drives us to another grey bunker. Light drops fast behind the mountains, dulling edges to lumps of buildings, open maw of trucks.

We could have walked, I say. It isn't far, but easy to get lost, Barney answers calmly, like he's answered dumb questions all his life. We hatch out like chicks, turned out into a grey hallway with pictures of miners and businessmen holding giant cheques, shaking hands, smiling, some baring their teeth. My father worked in a mill; reception area had the same pictures with the screech and hum of machines steady behind metal doors. Not allowed to go in there, he said. Sounded like animals, men taming them with instruments, steel ones with an edge.

A wiry man named Mark comes out to meet us, tells us he is an engineer with the mine, has been working there since the beginning. Must be ten years, he says, trying to surprise us, but his eyes are resigned. Delicate like a dancer, shorn hair, dark blue eyes, glint of old pain that doesn't reach his lips. Bobs a bit when he talks, like he is ducking swings. I will be doing your training, he announces and leads us into a darkened room, tables, chairs in a half-circle around a mounted TV and video machine. Our voices sound hollow, like air is being sucked out the door. Forms asking for our medical history, contact numbers. In case anything happens, he says as he slides in a video.

I apologize for the length—it's forty-five minutes but should have been twenty. Try not to sleep through the long bits. It's about what to do if you run into a bear. This is grizzly country. Have any of you had dealings with a bear? Diana raises her hand, says she was tracked once by a young black bear when she was on a dig. What did you do? Mark asks. Made noise all the way to the truck, she answers, and we laugh nervously. In the north, everyone grows up with bears, Rich says. Black bears trolled the dump when we were kids, I say. Sat in the truck and watched them overturn boxes, tear and slurp the bottoms, move on, could hear them snuffling. Few times they crossed a country road I was walking; we'd both stop, eye each other, wary silence.

I don't carry a gun when I'm in the bush, or bear spray, Mark says. Just let them know where I am. With that he leaves and we watch black bears, grizzlies, grunting in distress, running at people spliced into the film. They talk to the bears, say, Go away, bear, clap their hands, beat trees with a stick, climb on stumps and rocks and wave their arms. Back up slowly, don't turn around. Back up slowly, don't turn around. If a grizzly attacks, play dead, cover your head with your jacket, hands, arms, whatever is free; beat back a black bear, fight with your entire body, stick your fingers in their eyes.

Mark comes to get us, leads us back to the dining hall. Tables are wide and round, like furniture found in schools. The cook tells us about his life as he loads up our plates. He grew up by a lake in the north. Parents took him to town a few times a year to shop; he wanted everything. I'm from the north too, I say, but he talks over me, can't stop. Now he takes his kids to the Edmonton Mall; they love the rides and the pool—so much water in one place. It's the prairies, they don't have water like that anywhere. Glint in his eye, doesn't want to let us go. His helper is tall, carefully combed black hair; cleans off plates, mops the floors. I cannot even hear his footsteps.

Mark comes to our table, tells us to watch out for bears when we leave the dormitory in the morning. They hang out by the kitchen, seduced by the smells, startle people on their way out. Pack a lunch in a paper bag, he says. You'll be hungry. We pick at our food, dawdle in and out of conversation. Light is sharp with a brown edge, musty haze, though the room is spotless. Some men at other tables start a card game, I can hear the swift shuffling, scrape of chairs, snorts of laughter.

Diana spreads the map on the table, shows us Kemess Lake, so tiny, an ink blot, crowded by mountains and industry. Proposed conveyor belt line will follow the west side, an area that hasn't been explored in previous digs. We'll split up into two groups and start at either end, meet in the middle, see what we find. Diana, Jaclyn, Johnny and I will take the rough path in from the south, the least explored area. This is my first preliminary field reconnaissance; sounds like a military exercise, I say. Leaning over the map, spread-out decree of land lines inked in ochre, scratched pencil, I try to imagine myself within its boundaries, treading a new path hidden by dense scraping brush. Don't worry, you won't get lost, Johnny is with us, Irene laughs.

Some of us go to bed early, watch TV in our toasty rooms. It will be an early morning. Others play pool in the games room, loud '70s carpet, faux wood panelling. Miners didn't speak to the women, Rich told us the next day. Instead, they cornered him between painstaking shots, told him about their divorces, trips to Hawaii, new pickups with shiny spokes on the wheels.

> I struck, and struck again,
> And, growing still in stature, the huge Cliff
> Rose up between me and the stars, and still,
> With measur'd motion, like a living thing,
> Strode after me.

Six a.m. and the snow won't quit. Sky has reached down, scooped up the mountain in its cold hands, no line between the ground and its fists. I pound out of the door to scare the bear if there is one. There are scuffles in the rooms beside me but I am the only one at the table for coffee. Mark walks in and looks at my hiking shoes, says he has some boots that will do the trick, and as we leave, the rest straggle in, outfitted in hardy blues, Gore-Tex red and green. We hop in his truck to another shadowy building, walk through well-fortified rows of inventory, yellow coiled ropes, orange vests with myriad pockets, boxes of parts; well organized, no mess. Smells of oil and sweat. There are women that work here, not a lot but they come, he says. We have boots in all sizes. I find a pair that fits. Wet feet means a short day; he eyes me warily, pegging me for a city girl who will pack it in early.

Spends his days off out in the woods, unarmed, curious, he tells me. Bored of the male talk, drone of hockey on the wide-screen TV. In the winter he climbs a peak for six hours—I'll show you the one—with his snowboard strapped to his pack; flies down in six minutes. Such a long haul but it's worth it, no one else around. He's on the shutdown crew, one week in, one week out to keep sane. Darkness comes quick out here, he tells me as we walk back to the truck, so I read a lot, live for my son when I see him.

When we get back to the dining hall the group is ready, backpacks stuffed with extra gloves, hats, wrapped ham sandwiches. Bear spray in our pockets. We toddle off as if to a winter playground, already sweating as we squeeze into the trucks. Johnny strides in with his lunch in a garbage bag, slung over his shoulder. He knows the lake, hunted and fished here as a kid. When we are dropped off, he flies through the scree to the first pink ribbon that signals the start of the trail before we have even scrambled down the bank. But Diana waits, chats with the driver on the radio; I can see her breath in grey waves. There is a problem: the other truck got stuck in the snow climbing a steep hill, couldn't make it to the other side, so we're all going in together. We wait for the crew. It snows and snows, crystals condensing on my hat, slipping through to my scalp. Johnny strides back and forth, eager to get going. Long stick in his hand, he demonstrates to us that if you bang on trees, water shakes off, stops the drenching.

Eight of us spread out across the slant. Two skim the top, two skirt the lake and the rest of us hobble up and down the mossy crags, raw tearing branches. Pink line is steady to the middle, Mark says, then it fades halfway through. We'll have to watch for it. Johnny and Irene keep close to the trail that Johnny knows. That's where the traps will be, Irene says. Our people didn't veer off much from the trail. Right away she finds a cache: pale branches stashed by a tree. A deadfall trap. She kneels by it, moves the moss away, revealing the depth. A log would cover a baited trap house, while a forty-pound pole would be set, waiting to crush necks and spines. How old is it? I ask, and she says, It's old, all right. We find trees shorn of bark for precious cambium; misshapen trunks curl around the scar. Some were scraped with ancient tools, some were gnawed by porcupines. How do you tell the difference? I lean in, join the crowd while Diana takes a picture. Snow slides off the slick leaves, drips on our cheeks, red noses. Markings are different; you can tell the chew of teeth, wood torn instead of scraped. A scar heals eventually, Diana says. In time the trunk folds in and touches, slow embrace.

Noooo bears, Mark calls out as we continue, a chiming that ricochets warning down the valley like we are the enemies, the ones to watch out for. Bears are looking for a place to sleep now, Irene says. *Go to sleep*, she warbles as she climbs. *Go to sleep*. Someone is laughing, jumping from the scruff of snowed boulders to holes that explode in white skiffs. Those could be dens, Irene says, gives me an owl eye. We are making enough noise to scare off all living things and still my neck shivers, only hot part on my cold body. Johnny finds another deadfall and we gather around a heap of bent branches. Lake is grey and murky, same colour as the steel sky. Hard to imagine anything lives there. Before the mine, Johnny fished here, camped on its verdant edge, its bottom yielding up rainbow trout.

Across the lean lake, steep forested bank of a sharp, bald mountain leaning forward like it's coming at us. Lake steel grey and murky. This is the mountain, Mark says, gesturing with a quick arm stroke. Diana takes a careful picture; curious eyes pick out soft shapes, dark contours that become art. Sky and mountain look the same in the winter, Mark says. Don't know where the horizon meets; feel your way through. Out on the mountain, though, climbing and clawing your way up clears your head. Feel small and mighty, all at once. I think of sturdy-legged goats, whose domain we are plowing through on clumsy feet. Sheep and bears and moose, caribou, deer nimble through narrow ridges, leave footprints, scratched trees, the occasional kill.

Two hours in we stop for water. Who is cold and wants to head back? Rich asks. His back is killing him, has been all morning. Irene's feet are soaked and Maureen's knees crunch with each step. Johnny says nothing at first. He could walk the entire perimeter of the lake twice before we straggle to the end. Sturdy branch still in his hand, garbage bag slung, still full. Shielding a flame to light another smoke, he surprises us and heads back too. Diana, Mark, Jaclyn and I will continue on. Diana brings out a map and Mark says the line gets a lot harder to follow. Incline will scatter with boulders, shale, crumpled, broken trunks and branches blocking the path. Until now the hike has been steep but mossy, some bramble and blowdown. Grey beauty of the deep mountain lake where mammoths wallowed.

Johnny leads the group to the lakeshore. We'll tie our path through so you can follow on the way back, Rich says. Johnny will make a fire at the lake, find dried kindling underneath broad tree branches. Mark says he always does this, a fire to warm everyone and thank the lake, an offering. He will walk along the edge of a beaver dam, solid and smooth, as if poured from concrete, and paddle and whack the water with his hiking stick, disturbing the beavers' peace. They will come out fierce, slapping tails, circling the interlopers. Johnny will laugh, light a smoke and move on.

Diana and Jaclyn stay up high, just below the treeline, bare grey boulders, some clingy moss, sheer ice beneath the snow. Slip and swing through the space between lean trunks while Mark and I struggle through the rough middle, pointed black roots, sticks that poke through my blue shell. Legs and arms hauling up and over, up and over, slip and swing. Cold, wet hair stuck to my face, unfashionable helmet. Snow turns to sleet, then rain, gloom bends

morning to midday. I'm not trained to see, so I listen to Diana—
she explains what to look for, signs, scrapes, cultural depressions.
Ancient life that went on and on below us, deep time.

No bears, I call out in my foghorn voice. No bears, the crew
echoes back. No sign of them, Mark says. Just let them know
you're coming through, they'll let you pass. Trying to find the
next pink ribbon. I let my eyes go like I'm dreaming and then it
pops out—works every time, I tell him. Path doesn't stay hidden
for long. We zigzag, swearing. Mark starts singing "Roxanne" in
a raspy falsetto voice. I tell him that song was a huge karaoke hit
when I was in Japan, how everyone yowled out Rox-anne in exag-
gerated passion, laughing, clinking our unison drinks.

When were you in Japan? he asks. About ten years ago. Two
days before I left, I went to see the eagles, their proud white heads
dotting winter wet trees in Squamish. Combination of too much
wine and nerves had me puking on the side of the road—every
ten minutes my friends pulled over, cool air revived me while I
heaved. Nothing left but guts, nausea wouldn't go. Walking on
slithery banks of the cool stony river. Last year there were hundreds of eagles, someone said, people taking pictures, kids tossing
rocks in the water, plop and skip. People marking lines on paper
for each head, like they were keeping score. Next day my friends
packed me pale in a van, two giant suitcases stuffed with my life,
whittled down, compact, agonized over. Took me days to decide.
I checked everything in, destination Osaka. And I wanted to feel
relieved, mess of packing away, choosing this, not that, lists, lists,
details scratched in margins of paper stuffed in my purse. Strange
space between one life, next one unimaginable, a hole I could fall
through. Felt so good to get off the plane, move in a new world.

Have to keep moving, Mark says, and we call for the others, wait for a response. End of the lake coming into view, swamp
of dead yellow grass lies to rest, still hasn't absorbed the snow.
Shallow valley opens up, cupped hands palming the dirt, jagged
shards, water that's freezing at the edges. I wonder if there are

campsites down there, I say. We won't be going there, Mark adds. Our job is to stick close to the conveyor belt line that will rip this mountain up if it happens. Follow the money line, I say. Diana and Jaclyn have called down *Here*, clear voices in a space between lunging. We stop for water, shake the rain off like we own fur instead of skin. I strain to hear bird flutter, thump of startled grouse.

Where does all the money come from? I call out to the back of his head. We have established a kind of rhythm between walking, silence, singing, brief stops, terse words and some stories, cold, red fingers tucked into our gloves like claws. I don't know, he says, stops to assess the next gnarl we crawl over. Who knows where all the money comes from.

Diana and Jaclyn reach the end of the mountain edge, start the climb down. I see their flushed faces hovering in evergreen branches before I hear them. Mark and I have reached a clearing. Feels weird to stand steady on two feet, instead of clinging to some mountain that's trying to shake us off, I say. Yeah, it sure felt like it, Mark says. My pack is soaked, spare gloves dripping. Four of us stand in a circle, unwrapping ham sandwiches, peanut butter and jam. Mark doesn't eat, fuelled by other things. Did you see anything up there? I ask Diana. Not much, few CMTs, culturally modified trees that have been scraped or blazed to mark trails. Snow's covered stuff; sure we missed things but we'll be back in the spring. Sky clears bluish grey, stronger sense of light, time passing. Half an hour break and a full stomach, the hollow that is filled paid for in numbing cold. I can hardly get my gloves back on.

Have to keep moving. We follow Diana through two metres of new-growth spruce. Air smells of fresh green, decay, tang of dirt. We've lost her until she calls *No bears*, understorey tripping us up again. We haul up a steep bank to a rough patch of road and then to a black tumble of avalanche boulders, sharp edged, broken, some worn smooth, obliterating the path. Covered with snow, they're treacherous. Skittering across, we catch glimpses of the mountain that the conveyor is heading to, the next mountain to be demolished. Instead of an open pit, the ore will be pulled out of the side, hollowed out like stuffing pulled from a pillow. Diana says, It's three o'clock; good enough. We lurch to a stop and pick a path down the black frozen waves.

Sun comes out to warm bits of skin and cheeks before it hides out again with some jealous peak. Thin ice sheets are plaiting the end of the lake. This is where the moose would be, if there were any, I say. Having reached our destination, fulfilled our duty, we start chatting again, no longer grim and silent. Pick through the mud and dead grass, find a caribou trail with deep, deep holes. Let's follow this, Mark says, and he is gone, quick as a colt. Just before we see the purple ribbon, smell of smoke drifts by. Four of us stand quiet. Johnny's fire for the lake, I say. He knows this place. That's why he doesn't need anything, everything is here.

At the other end of the lake, there is a cabin that has been there for hundreds of years. A hearth that burns down, down past the thin layer of dirt we see. So much below that won't be found. Torn roots of a toppled tree stop Diana. This is where you find stuff, she says, leaning in, yellow jacket smeared with shafts of blond hair. All our hair looks dark now, like the wet has revealed new skin chafing under the old. Sometimes you see points, traps, dangling from the roots like ornaments. Not this one though. We plunder on, sticking closer to the water, which gives more light. Cold and sore, a kind of lightness sets in my bones—how it feels at the end of something hard, anticipation of release.

Grind of massive wheels from the loaders accompanies our sprawling group as we emerge—last expanse of dead tree and bramble and the final pink ribbon leads us through the gravel to the road. Six hours ago the stones were covered in snow, now they are slick and mottled. We slog in for the last hundred metres in silence and climb the muddy bank up to the road, stand there side by side. Mark radios Rich to come pick us up. Feel like the freaking Tin Man, Diana says. Slow and creaking, I can hardly move. Triumph that we've made it shows in our smiles in the picture

Rich takes of us, though I didn't feel it. It sank in later, warm glow mixed in with fatigue, bruises revealing new lands traced on my body.

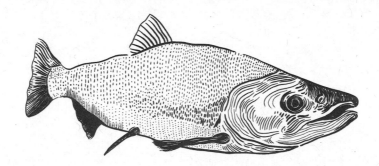

5

Lava Lake

Gingolx

Onion Lakes

Kitwanga River

Kaien Island

Kitkatla

Cabin Sites, Skeena River

Fish Camp, Skeena River

Lava Lake

Nisga'a Highway, narrow twisting road that winds around silver lakes. Thickets of trees unruly on both sides, raw tips of mountains like gates you pass through. Sign for Lava Lake, thirty kilometres, Nisga'a Memorial Lava Bed Park just past it. Two hundred fifty years ago an eruption levelled the land, buried two villages. Story is that some Nisga'a kids were taunting salmon, torturing them with sharp sticks. Centre of the earth poured forth, thick with retribution, wiped out even the memory of salmon for a while. Now it is a park. Fresh layer of earth still simmering down, down where the children played by a stream.

At Rosswood on Kalum Lake, I stop for a coffee at the General Store, local hangout and tourist dream. Warm wood interior, free-trade coffee, wide counter where fresh cinnamon buns sell every morning. I've missed them today but the sweet smell lingers. Buckwheat noodles, spelt, lemon basil balsamic vinegar. Little plastic bags of trail mix with bright M&Ms. Do you have a washroom? I ask the handsome man at the till, greying reddish beard. I wonder if he lives in the yurt I saw outside of town, long grey planks bent to geometric forms, like living in an outdoor cave. We have an outhouse just outside, he says. There's hand sanitizer on the front porch. Easy smile, he fills up the mugs of two older men chatting at a nearby table.

Lakes circle mountains like moats, swampy shores, no cars ahead or behind. Road rises higher. Lava Lake emerges to my left, narrow and glistening, road hugging its steep sides. Mountain lake deep, more long than wide, squeezed by rough-edged peaks. Bottom black like tar. To my right, first glimpse of the lava swells, black and dull grey with a skin of beige lichen. Each monstrous wave formidable, cracks emit stones the size of car engines, jutting like broken bones. A pull-off shows a trail to where the eruption began and I start out, crunching on the black pebbles. Just me and the wind, space wide like an open mouth that swallowed the humans so long ago. Lurching lava rolls on either side. Brave trees with slender stalks climb out of the black cracks. I hear a crash in the bush just past the trail. Early spring and bears are everywhere; I saw cubs by the side of the road, watching cars with wide eyes. I turn back, not wanting a chance encounter with their mother.

As I pull out to the highway, satellite radio loses its signal. It has been intermittent for a while but now the silence from outside seeps in. I decide to ride it, coast like a wave. Slough off some dead parts. Road swerves through a widening grey lake of lava, green of the encircling forest receding, leaves shimmering in the wind. I reach the turnoff to New Aiyansh and Gingolx. Black lava has engorged the entire valley. Two rows of mountains preside like kings at court, watching over the land as it tries to regrow, tree by weary tree, through craters, holes, jagged cracks.

There are pull-offs on the way to Gingolx and I get out at each one. Tourist season has not hit its stride, so it's just me. At first I feel forsaken, like I'm the last straggler, the one who wasn't saved. Silence is oppressive. I walk down the exposed paths and scurry back to my car as if being chased. I get braver, walk farther, jump into craters I can climb out of, hop over deep fissures where I can't see all the way down. Wind doesn't seem to want to strike me down. Whiz of the occasional car, no one looks to see. When I let the wind move me, I become a pilgrim, treading the stones with attention. Moss grows from beige to light green, kind of fuzz, a sprouting skin. Some areas are flatter, more foliage, like the rock is becoming ground again. A new layer, the next bottom. Centuries from now this could be the sea. Huge swaths are impassable. I stand on the side of the road and look out at the chunks of grit, spew of earth. How it must have burned everything in sight when it emerged.

A friend walked out on the lava, on her own pilgrimage, and came across a wolf. Tall, lean, brownish grey, she said, and so still. They watched each other from a distance in that great expanse, each mirroring the movement of the other for some time. Like the lava was water, a reflection wavering in the afternoon light. She is passionate about wolves and it was like she met herself there in the wide ancient trough, she said. Met her spirit and what moves her. Lava is like another plane, like traversing the past, the dream world, and the very real. You can meet yourself there in what comes out to greet you.

Lava is rough, I was cautioned. Don't wear flip-flops. It'll cut through your jeans if you fall, tear your skin. When I pick up a stone it is porous and warm, chafing in my hands. I add a large chunk to a pile that is slowly being constructed by tourists, a kind of shabby pyramid. Sticks of dead wood are laid out in a dried bed of grass like splayed bones of a small deer, its delicate jaw curved, stubs of branches like small teeth. Wind whips through the valley, a cleansing cull, shooing away remnants. I heard a bird but did not see one make the long flight across the dark ground. Valley has seen me and shown me its rough beauty, how it is still evolving, its presence growing, becoming its own thing.

I stop at the grocery store at New Aiyansh for more water. New building with a café and post office, all under construction. Three aisles of all-white shelves are empty and the aisle closest to the front is packed with Cracker Jack. Coolers full of pop. Glass display with deep-fried chunks in metal plates. An old man is leaning in close, making his choice. A man and a woman stand uncertainly by the doors, peering out. My footsteps echo on the way to the washroom. An older man is talking intently to a stout man with paint-splattered vest and boots. I guess he is the restaurant owner by his serious gaze. Where is the food? a young girl asks her mother as they walk in. The girl is in pink, wide eyed.

Lava ends if you go far enough. Past the turnoff to Gitwinksihlkw, Nass River nips in, brings green with it. Road is crowded by a lush valley. A mother moose crosses, a racing calf behind her. A truck stops and the driver and I exchange wonder. Did you see that? I told him that I had just wandered the lava beds. Did you see the cone? he asks. Like a huge funnel into the earth. It's on the tour if you take it. He and his wife are from Australia. Their faces glow with excitement, telling me what I've missed.

Ahead is a pull-off for the hot springs. Last time I was here there was no sign and a muddy path with ropes over ancient stumps to get to a small pool ringed with cedar. Now there is a new sign, brown with white letter engraving, a cleared parking lot, a wooden walkway through a swamp, a change room, three pools with high wooden sides. I change quickly and go to the hottest pool. A young family bobs in one corner, bearded dad, tattooed mom and squealing young daughter in her arms. Smell of sulphur strong in the spring air, patch of mottled sky overhead, steep muddy banks and towering trees. I ease into the almost scalding water, so dark it swallows my limbs, stretch out, hold myself up on my elbows. Bottom is a skein of mud and plastic; my feet skid across the surface. Constant trickle of a stream, nattering voices, steady stream of visitors. New sign has done its work. Water works its magic, minerals and mud clean pores, lighten spirit. Spring survived the eruption, just on the edge of where the lava stopped.

There is a fishing camp near the Nass, blue tarps flapping and trucks parked near the rocky banks, hiding secret fires and ways. There is a mound of yellow stones just past it, crumbling like a once grand pyramid. Enticed, I pull over and get out, combat the crouching silence. Scramble the sides, looking for a shard that grabs me. Maybe it is the shimmer of gold, how it glows with promise, blares out from all the green. What is it with the sky that unfolds on this place, how I want to take a piece or replace what has been taken. Stone for stone.

Gingolx

Road climbs the steep rocky outcrops and dips down to wide grassy bays where eagles line up, each to its own tree stump. Watching the waves. Nass runs into salty Portland Inlet; somewhere out there it is mixing, fresh and salt water, seals slipping through for some salmon. Turns are sharp, slowing and accelerating like a carnival ride. A porcupine, its quills rippling and golden in the spring light, waddles with authority down the yellow line and slowly veers to the shoulder. We slow to its speed and it keeps going, doesn't glance our way.

At the restaurant, the owner tells us of the grizzly that can stop traffic for hours. It can flip your car in an instant, so you have to wait him out, he says. Grizzly owns the road. Restaurant is empty except for us, my parents and me, but is festive, coloured lights framing the doorway and windows. Faded pictures of tourists holding giant salmon, pale halibut, beaming at the camera. The owner is in some of them, friendly smile. His wife and he have been running the restaurant for years, serving halibut and chips to tourists, he says. Their easy banter warms the place. Outside, moss-covered houses squeeze in tight to the rocks, like they were built from them. Hard to imagine anything getting them out. Road wasn't even paved until we got the treaty twenty years ago, he says and fills our coffee. We hunkered in all winter, had all the food we needed, didn't see anyone else for months.

Ocean beckons us and we walk to where the sand smooths. Rocks glistening with moss and bulbous kelp; we try not to slip. There is a concrete walk along the bay, two or three rows of houses stacked behind the main road, some roofs coated with thick moss. Playsets in front yards. Portland Inlet stretching silver and black around treed islets. On maps it is enormous. I keep that image to remind me we are seeing just one ancient view. How far is Alaska? Dad asks. Wonder if we're looking at it. He avoids the sharp rocks of the shore, waits for us on a log.

Place is protected, I say, so hard to get here, tucked into the rocks. Weathered totem poles, raven beaks and slanted wings, faces of men and children whose stories are inscribed, uncovered by the salt air. They look past us to the sea. How many people have pushed off from this beach to the sea, not knowing what they would find or if they would come back? A young woman wanders the boardwalk with two small children. Maybe they come here every day, rhythm of life slow here, steady like the tides. Timeless weather and seasons passing, a kind of constancy worn into the wood, the stones, the rows of homes in neat lines.

A man comes up to us, skinny in a jean jacket. Hey, do you want to see my paintings? Something urgent in his eyes. Sure, I say. We're here visiting. I'm Gitxsan but I live here now, he says. I'm Bobby. He nods as we introduce ourselves. Been here a long time, he says. Dark grey hair to his shoulders. My paintings are in there, I'll show them to you. His eyes dart over us, out to the boardwalk and back. Thin face both hungry and avid. He gestures to an imposing cedar hall, steep roof and thick logs holding up each corner. Wide doors painted in red and black whales, smooth bodies leaping. This is the feast hall, he says. I can show you. He rattles the door but gives up. I'll go get a key, he says and runs down an alley.

We stand uncertainly in front of the feast fall and Bobby runs up to us, trailed by a short, round man with a string of keys around his neck. He has the keys to the whole town, Bobby says. The man introduces himself as Joseph, tells us that Bobby tracked him down at the house, saying some people want to see his paintings. So here he is, Bobby says, leading us to the hall. Joseph unlocks the two heavy doors and Bobby leaps into the building. This is our feast hall, Joseph says. I'm the fireman here, so I have keys to every building. He is mild mannered, unsurprised to have his day interrupted by Bobby, by us. Every year we gather here to feast and dance, for days on end, Joseph says. People from the other villages come here, other parts of BC and Alaska, and some years, we go to their village. Bobby points to his painting, a wolf as tall as he is. Its thick red tongue licking the edges of its lips. Whole inside of the building is golden cedar, each panel painted in white, black and red. It takes a while for the spirits to take shape. I stand in front of each one and the features appear, bear, raven, salmon, killer whale.

Bobby shows us every painting in the hall. See what they did here? he says, pointing to thick lines and strokes that formed the base of skulls, a wide row of teeth, a tail. The ones he painted and didn't paint. His thin wrists flowing over the figures as if painting them again. Movements jittery still but he is less nervous. He speaks with authority, knows the story of each animal. Joseph stands at the doorway, light spreading his shadow wide across the wide-planked floor.

Onion Lakes

I follow Leah in her Range Rover with no working signals. Roads are wet; clouds swallow the top of a range we pass through, headlights threading through the murk. Coming down from the pass, it's daylight again, but shrouded, like the sky is holding something back, a sly sleight of hand.

Remo, her pit bull, tears out of the back seat. Leah and Natalie slip on their packs, toques, gloves. Rain pants, jackets, insulated rubber boots. North coast winter walks are a slog through slush, pelting rain, the occasional wicked wind. We analyze the map that marks the trail. There're three lakes; path circles them all like black stitches. I guess they look like onions, Natalie says. Look more like squashed grapes to me, she adds. We start on the path: mud, dry earth covered in spruce needles, clear ice like lacquer. Hemlocks thick and straight witness our walk, bark hanging like loose, scaly skin. At the base of some trunks are holes where sap pooled, then froze, yellow like cooled honey. I read somewhere that the sap can be used as an antibiotic cream, Leah says. Warm brown eyes, kind face, her voice conspiratorial.

Both Natalie and Leah are massage therapists; bodies are their medium. Chests, shoulders, complaining hips, they give up a lot of secrets, Leah tells me, if you listen. Remo has spotted another dog ahead on the trail. He stands stock still, that moment before the furious run. Some people flop on my table and ask me to heal them and they keep coming back, asking why they're not healed. I just worked at resorts and spas, Natalie says. Bodies in and out all day, like factory parts, slapped together to make a person.

We start down a steep switchback that leads to the first lake. We slow at the treacherous corners, skid down to the shore. Water looks black, reflecting the grey sky, edged with snow, limbs of trees jutting from the shallows. Path follows the edge and the water is clear, bottom strewn with rocks, branches, stones, all covered in rich brown silt. Mist drifts low through the evergreens. Lake small like a breath you hold for a moment.

Trail leads us to a sturdy bridge crossing a stream, clear mountain water over a creek bed of sharp-edged boulders. Waist-high lime-green spruce pop up from the shore, frame the creek. Stillness reminds me of mountain streams in Japan. Path follows the stream that connects to the next lake. No snow, just the soft thump of our boots, rushing water. Natalie tells us about a chance for her to work in Inuvik for the summer. If I go to a place that holds me, I'll stay, but until then, I'm fine with change, she says.

We clamber up and over stumps and roots; trail is not steady. Silence of trees accompanies us. Second lake is smaller, covered in snow, hard to see where the edge is. Sky still has not lifted. At the farthest lake, the smallest, the coldest, a strange quiet descends on us. Remo continues his charging ahead and back. I know a story about a man who lives on a lake like this, Natalie says. You know, odd men who live on little no-place lakes like this hatch plots to end the world, can't be caught by the cops or anyone. Everyone's heard of someone, Leah says. It's kind of a generic story now. Strange how my niece started talking about hermit bombers at around the same place on this lake, she continues. Chill of that thought lingers. Doesn't look like anyone's living here, I say, though something about the lake lends itself to dark stories, especially on a day when the sky is hugging in too tightly.

Kitwanga River

On the road to Gitanyow a wolf runs across the road, a flash of dark, sudden and black. Kyle was sure it was a wolf. Way too big to be a coyote. I had never seen a wolf, still wasn't sure I had. We whipped past the spot where we saw it and not even a branch shivered. Maybe it was a ghost, I say. Eyes can play tricks on you this early in the morning.

We left Orenda Camp at 7 a.m.; nowhere to stop for a quick coffee from here to Kitwanga, where the Petro-Can sells bannock and Twizzlers side by side. Another couple of hours to Gitanyow for the job fair that starts at 10 a.m. We'll have plenty of time to set up, Kyle says, slurping his coffee, confident; he's done this before. I want to see the totem poles, I say. Sure, we can do that, it's on the way, he says. Lots of them by the river. He is looking for a country station on the radio but we're stuck with the drone of CBC. Kyle's face creased and lined, eyes faded blue, dull white and watery, as if they were used to being submerged. His face reminds me of a turtle, slow to smile, steady eyed, but he speaks at the speed of his thoughts, an unmitigated rush, like a river busting through embankments.

Orenda Camp was a string of 1980s trailers, motley park just off the Alaska Highway. It had been around for a long time, housing government employees laying out blocks along rutted forest service roads. In the winter the pipes freeze and no one goes near it until spring. Each year you hold your breath when you walk through the door, Kyle says. Narrow forest service roads thread out from the highway, snake in and out of the woods, but you can see the wide muddy Nass if you get out at the higher spots, he says.

Land feels higher here, like we are driving slowly to the sky, scraping the tops and sides of trees. Colder, *more north*, like the magic books with pages of goblins dancing in the forest when you were a kid. Mountains to the north are ice capped year-round, house glaciers and mining camps where young men who live in the Okanagan fly to, two weeks in, two weeks out. I've met them on planes. Wouldn't dream of living here, a young mining engineer told me on a flight to Prince George. Listening to rap, loud and thumping beside me, his shoulders rolling to the rhythm. Can't wait to get back to civilization.

Two couples live full-time in Orenda Camp, but we meet only one. Kyle says the other couple spend most of the time inside, drinking and watching sports on TV. When they do venture out, they squint in the light like groundhogs poking their heads out. Seeing if it's summer yet. Lou and Brenda, the other couple, are from the Lower Mainland, came up twelve years ago. Kyle says they're always around. Lou is tall and bald with stained work overalls, his name tag over his right pocket. Gentle voice, friendly face, like your favourite uncle. He gives us a tour of his huge garage, tools meticulously arranged on three-metre walls. Insulated, heated, lighted, used year-round, clean and silent like an operating room. I get music piped in here, he says, pointing to speakers hanging from the raftered ceiling. Bob Seger, the Eagles, whatever I feel like at the time. Life is way better up here, he says, hands Kyle and me a beer. No one around to bother you. Lou clears the highway of snow in the winter, drives huge plows and graders. Maintains them in a lot beside his trailer. I listen to Soundgarden when I'm fixing things, he says. It seems to fit.

We are standing in the gravel road that links the row of trailers together. Road loops around like a racetrack. Across from us, away from the highway, a long, low building that houses a kitchen/mess area, some more trailers, for when the camp runs full bore, which it doesn't much anymore. Logging isn't what it was now that the cream is gone, Lou says, but there's enough to keep the locals going. It's May, so snow has just eased off, camp area brown, rutted and raw, like a glacier has just moved off after a century. I imagine it how it used to be, thriving, people from the south, east, the US. Looking for a fortune, breaking the land and leaving. Voices rising and falling in the mess hall, rumble of trucks, always the trucks. Some men way out in the bush who come in once a week, eyes glazed from lack of sleep and too much time alone. And the women, where were the women? I look for the signs.

Brenda joins us with a cat in her arm, coffee mug steaming. Sun has just come out to flash in her eyes, glare off her glasses. Can't tell by her expression if she's happy to see us. Do you want to see my chickens? she asks me and bounds across the muddy road in her rubber boots, looking back to see if I'm following. Short dark hair, tightly layered around her round face, shaved at the neck. Flowing plaid shirt and black jeans. I follow her, realizing that she's still talking to me over her shoulder. Lou built me the chicken coop our second winter here, when I was going crazy for something to do, she says. Really missing my kids and wanted to look after something, you know? Keep things alive. I got three hens for eggs, then we got some chicks; now I have twenty. Only name the ones I'm going to keep.

At the gate into the chicken coop, painted a cherry red with white trim—by far the brightest thing in Orenda Camp—she stops and looks at me. Brown eyes sharp, intent. No questions as to why I was standing in the road. Knowing she is the curiosity, the person who lives with her husband and chickens in the middle of nowhere. I don't ask how it is at Orenda, or why she's here. Coop is hot and dark, like how I'd imagine a cave in India, somehow a holy place. In a little fenced yard, she introduces me to Zelda, Lulu, Carol and Susie. White and fluffy, well fed, they still make a run for it as she closes the gate. Coop doesn't smell like chickens, straw fresh and crunchy. It's like a petting zoo, I say. Brenda gives a tight smile and leads me out into the light.

Dip in the road and we turn off to Gitanyow, alongside the Kitwanga River. Roll down my window, water grey and rushing, banks swathed in long grass. Main road leads us past the totem poles and we pull in by the museum. We have some time before we have to set up, Kyle says, lights up a smoke by the truck. Parking lot pocked and muddy, museum closed. Sun breaking through chunks of cloud, glaring and then hiding. I stop at each totem pole, examine its curves. One figure holds a small child in its wide hands carved in its chest. Touch of white in the child's eyes, hand in its mouth. Adult hands holding the child in place, protecting and leading forward. Weathered now, some streaks of red around the lips, black-lined eyes.

At the school gym we set up the table left for us by a steep row of bleachers. Gym that doubles as a community hall, theatre, gathering place. Hard to imagine a basketball game here, nets raised like gangway planks. Other vendors are piecing together their displays, unrolling posters, setting out boxes of pens, brochures with smiling faces, some of them Indigenous, with hard hats and high-vis vests, standing in green fields, in mining pits, in helicopters. We have signs and posters and handouts, dark green stripes with fine print. Corporate communications with young men and women smiling, surrounded by trees and machines. Forestry jobs are the way to go, Kyle says. When LNG is done, there will always be trees. He has been a forester for twenty-five years, knows the ropes. Knows that foresters like the bush, not necessarily people, but he got good at that too. Lots of people have logging experience out here, he says, layout, cruising, but not the schooling behind it.

There are two liquefied natural gas companies and three mining companies from what I can see. Young men from the community are crowding them, asking questions, handing over resumés. An RCMP booth is attended by two young cops slumped and uncomfortable in tiny metal chairs. Older Japanese couple, dressed in linen pants and suit jackets over wool sweaters, are selling golden jars of honey made from local hives. They hand out honey-flavoured suckers to the swarm of kids at their table, delicate smiles on their faces. Rest of us are in jeans, respectable sweaters, high rubber boots to combat the spring muck.

Lucinda, one of the organizers, comes around to each table with bagged lunches. We'll be starting pretty soon, she says, long dark hair and bright smile. An Elder, swathed in a red and black button blanket, outline of a frog in shiny abalone, walks over to a microphone set up in the middle of the room. Wide face, grey hair sloped over her forehead, black-rimmed glasses. Head poking out like a small bird from its nest, taking a cautious look around. In a strong voice she speaks her language. No one else speaks. Then she welcomes us in English, her hands rising at her sides like wings. Our people need work, she says, voice slow, building up to something, but then it cracks. There is a beat of silence and then she walks away from the microphone and Lucinda steps in.

I've done forestry, laid out blocks, a few years back, Wesley says, handing me his resumé, his hair parted in the middle, thick and black. Heavy-set in a jean jacket, he looks me in the eye, levels with me. I want to stay here, he says, so if you have anything, give me a call, and he moves on, handing his resumé to the next table. More men like him come, some older, some with lots of experience in the bush. I want a labour job, Thomas says, so I can save to buy a car. He is eighteen in saggy jeans and a silver chain necklace, so young, looks lost in his down jacket. I want to go to Vancouver, live with my aunt, see what the city is like.

After we pack up, we drive around the village, up and down the gravel roads, past the school, the health centre with its paved slanted entry, the band office, which is small and looks like a repurposed cabin. Past some trailers that were makeshift fisheries and lands and resources offices. Village just shaking itself off from winter, before the spring rains come to flush out the dead grass, the leaves piled up at the end of driveways. Two kids cut across a grassy field toward the one store in town, its Open sign glowing a cheery pink. He is stolid with slow steps; she skitters in front, runs back, cajoles him. Some dogs tied up, some lying in slivers of sun.

Kaien Island

Leah is in the back, our guide, keeper of snacks and valuables. Huge Nikon hangs from her neck; in her bag, lenses to focus in on the smallest things. She wants to taste the sea, she tells us. It has been on her mind. Prince Rupert is on the coast, protected by bridges as mountain passes, she says as I follow Highway 16 through Terrace, past Shames Mountain and toward the Pacific. Kaien Island, where the Butze Rapids are, is the only place that has beaches.

Natalie points to a black wall of sky ahead, blotting out the weak spring sun. Big wet drops splash the windshield and transform into a waterfall, obscuring the road for minutes at a time. We plow on. It is the coast, after all, Leah calls from the back. In between breaks in the rain, I spot cars parked on the shoulder off the highway, along the Skeena. Sea lions swim up the Skeena to feast on oolichan this time of year, Leah says. Follow the flocks of seagulls and that's where they'll be.

In some places the riverbed is so low there are dark figures perched on the lip of the river, elaborate tripods set up, wilfully ignoring the rain, the squawking gulls. Homing in for the perfect shot of sea lion pods. So sea lions can survive out of sea water then? I ask Leah but she is pointing to a rest area just ahead.

We struggled into our rain gear, tie the hoods so the wind doesn't blow water in our faces. Scramble to the rocky edge and peer into the grey afternoon. I see sleek heads glistening on the surface, grey and shining. Leah spots them in her camera but they disappear. We passed some on sandbars, I glimpsed their huge bodies, thick and grey as boulders, but there are none at this spot. We stand in soaked silence and then head back to the car.

When we reach the parking lot of Kaien Island, grey and

white balls of clouds bound across the washed blue sky. Map of the island at the trailhead shows the trail following its perimeter. Should take a couple of hours, Leah says, then we'll have a late lunch. We are immediately enveloped in green, moss dripping from thin branches, spread luxuriously over boulders, long-dead trees like extra padding to muffle out the world, protect some inner workings, rough edges. Green sucks in the light and layers it out in leaves, thick hemlock and cedar stumps. Leah tells us there are wolves that roam the island, attack dogs if they can lure them off the trail.

Trail is wide and well gravelled, leading up and down steep ravines, across well-built bridges that will soon ford streams. Snow is still holding back the rush and the silence cloaks us in an extra skin, lets us soak in the water in the air, green coming out of our pores. In the middle of the island is a clearing like the sheared top of a head—boggy in spots, with tufts of dead grass and stubborn bushes. Must have logged this a while back, Natalie says as the wind whips at our legs, lashes hair into our eyes, our mouths. Weather-worn bench lonely in the field, with a plaque to commemorate a loved one, who loved this spot for its rough beauty. All around us are mountains rounded by the water, green in parts and shorn in others, odd patchwork of harvesting. How do they even get to those places, I say. No one knows. We hurry out of the unwelcome exposure like darting animals, back into the green lusciousness where we lose ourselves again.

Butze Rapids separate the island from the mainland. Knots of swirling whitewater as wide as a truck twist in so tight, foam bubbles up from the bottom like a cauldron. At the centre the water smooth and ropy, glistening like the glow of a grey eye. A group of kayakers, strapped tight in their vessels, black helmets, orange life jackets, flashing oars that look like toothpicks from the viewpoint. They're holding them up like tightrope walkers do, working hard to stay still as they traverse the chasm beneath. Some of them can't hang on and they spin out across the narrows, caught by the swirling current coming at them, bottom reaching up. We go down to where the waves roll, on the edge of mossy rocks, roar of combustion. Continuous glossy curve, wave up to my shoulder, rolling over and over on itself. Unnerving, standing so close to such power, fuelled by push and pull of the sea. Could snatch us away, so we stand back, salt spray on our faces a warning.

I would love to try that out, Natalie says, her eyes glowing, and Leah and I laugh at her. No freaking way I would, I say and Leah agrees. Beaches spread out beside us as we follow the trail loop. Musk of sea stronger in some places. Leah has her taste and says it's not as salty as she expected, remembering a time when the taste stayed with her for days. She gathers rocks, examines each one carefully and keeps the ones that warm her hands. Maybe they came from the centre of the earth, that's why they still glow now, I say. Natalie and I eat our snacks, watch another storm cloud roll in. Where the sea meets the island there's a watching place, looking for storms to come, people to come back from the sea.

Kitkatla

Four of us load into the Beaver float plane at Seal Cove in Prince Rupert, two in the middle row, Mick in the back and me in the front, strapped in. Tiny storage area behind Mick stuffed with bags, flats of food for the village. Pilot does a rote review of safety features, where to find the life jackets. Don't inflate them until you're out of the plane, he says. Reddish-brown hair with a beard, not young or old, gruff manner on the edge of annoyed. We buckle up, stuff in earplugs. Beaver engine roars as we taxi out. Ducks and geese skim the water, otter pops its head, dives back in. We drift off the ocean into the air, smooth as if water lifted to see us off. Wings lightly battered by the wind and we circle out and south to Kitkatla.

We pass Prince Rupert harbour, giant freighters anchored offshore like drifting icebergs, other freighters loading up with containers. Mounds of coal shaped in neat black piles line up by rows of railcars. Aside from a few patches of colourful maritime houses, machines rule the landscape: loaders, cranes, bulldozers, sides of yellow and red, thick black lettering. Cruise ships dock here on their way to Alaska; tourists wander the quaint shops of Cow Bay, eat fresh fish, buy Prince Rupert souvenirs. I've wandered the area on my own, eaten sushi made by Japanese chefs flown up from Vancouver. The business is saving us, Mick told us before we boarded. He lives in Prince Rupert, has lived on Haida Gwaii. A businessman and local logger with an air of authority, constantly on his phone or computer, even during meetings.

We pass over a strip of rough water and we're travelling low over steep, treed islands. Lines of clear-cut logging etched high up the mountainsides, signs from the old bad days when there were no obligations to plant, look after the environment.

Everything is tightly controlled now, Mick says. He'll make a point of telling the Chiefs, who are still angry at the mess that has been left. We fly over swamps and patches of little lakes, land striated and scratched out by glaciers. Looks rocky and bare but there are deer and wolves hidden in the trees, in the low dense bushes. I lean in for a closer look but we swerve off again. This is Porcher Island below us, Mick calls out to all of us. I looked at a map when I knew I was coming. Porcher is the largest in a series of smaller islands. Kitkatla is on a smaller one, Dolphin Island, chosen for its protected cove, its access to food. It has been inhabited for 8,500 years.

Mick is tall and imposing with grey hair and light blue eyes. He is leading our team of loggers and foresters to begin logging on Kitkatla territory. Licence is owned by the Gitxaala Nation, a big step, but the Chief and Council, Hereditary Chiefs and the community need to be informed. It's a big change for the community, he says, as they are traditionally fishermen. I represent the government; the operations manager and supervisor of his logging contractor, Jeff and Steve, are coming to explain the operations side. They'll be asking about jobs, Mick says, has been saying since we met. Make sure they get some jobs.

Village comes into view. Neat rows of rectangle houses placed where the longhouses used to be. Spire of a church in the middle. I find out later it was built by a Japanese architect, who came to the island to stay while it was built, ensuring his vision came to be. There's a road leading to a sewage lagoon, another to a graveyard. Aside from these roads and buildings, the island is bush and trees with little knobs of hills that would take a few hours to climb. Landing is not as smooth as takeoff; wind has whipped up whitecaps. We taxi in to a dock swaying in the waves. A middle-aged man with thick black hair, slight paunch, hazard vest, greets us as we disembark. You're stuck here now, he says with a smile. He chats with the pilot, who confirms that the wind may prevent the afternoon pickup. But you're not totally stuck, he says as we walk up the gangway. A ferry is coming in this afternoon.

There's a bus waiting, driven by a friendly older man, but we decide to walk. Dock is packed with boats, mainly fishing schooners, metal pulleys and ropes strewn on decks, stacks of traps. In a rocky bay behind the dock are wrecks of old boats, left to slowly dismantle into the sea. Wind cuts through my thin jacket, smears our hair in our faces. Mick is leading us to the learning centre, where we'll meet Joan and her team, get ready for our presentation. Jeff, chipper and fit, keeps up with Mick, asks him questions. Steve, softer and sullen, walks with me.

Main administrative office sits on the rocky shore, whole wall of windows reflects the grey day. Community hall beside it looks like an old theatre, with a rounded facade like a marquee. It has been here the longest, built before the Depression, Mick says. Joan greets us with a big hello, girlish laugh, brown eyes wide behind dark-framed glasses. Blond hair and white mixing in, can't tell the difference. She bustles around us, take-charge energy easing us in. Amanda, quiet and shielded in the corner, smiles sideways at us. Room set up for class, long tables and plastic chairs, Joan at the front, fielding questions. When do we meet the Chiefs? White spring light streams through the window, with views of the brown block of school, looking official in cedar doors and window frames. Kids squealing in the playground at recess, riding bikes on the road. Kitkatla all around us and I want to see it. But first the Chiefs.

A man is talking as we walk in. Rows of community members, Hereditary Chiefs among them, watch us file to our seats. Black-framed glasses and white hair, soft voice introduces us to silence. We say our piece. There are questions about how the land is still recovering from thirty years ago. How are we going to be different? Each Chief has their say. We are ocean people, an old man says, rising carefully from his chair. Tall and stooped, brown leather jacket, drooping white moustache. Everyone stops to listen. We are ocean people and we depend on the sea, he says, and that will never change. A table laden with sandwiches and soup,

seaweed and cookies is set up for lunch and we load up plates, eat
on our laps. Soft chatter around us. How did it go? Jeff asks and
Mick says really well but we don't believe him.

After the meeting we spill out of the large entrance to the
afternoon sunshine, the constant wind, chatting with members of
the community. Rose has lived in Prince Rupert and Vancouver and
has come back, long dangly earrings, short brown hair. Standing by
her husband, sweeping crumbs off his cuffs. Tyson, the computer
person at the learning centre, shy beside me. Flow of people with
bags of food in their hands like after a wedding or a party.

There is only enough room on the plane back for the men and Joan
coaxes me to stay, take the plane out in the morning. We'll call to
make sure you get a seat, she says as we head out of her classroom
toward the house she stays in. You can see the ocean out the back
porch, have coffee out there if you like. She knows everyone, stops
every few feet to chat, introduce me. Warm smiles and hugs, nods
in my direction. Young mothers showing their children's sleeping
faces. Elders out for walks, a few with canes, deep in conversation,
barks of laughter. Church painted white with green trim, inset
stained-glass windows like diamonds, sign of the cross over the
door, a cross at the top, simple and gold coloured. Smell of sea
through everything, tang of salmon as we pass the village smokehouse. Joan takes me to visit the crafting house, painted dark
brown with wide windows. Group of women bent over beading,
deep focus, room packed with bags of scraps and materials, kettle
just boiling. I've been coming here for two years now, Joan says.
I scramble to keep up with her brisk walk. I stay for months in
the winter when it's too hard to get out, she tells me, direct gaze.
Don't you feel a bit trapped, I ask, like you need to get out? I'm
already feeling a bit antsy, the town before us compact but porous,
all kinds of worlds seeping in.

Three little girls playing in the front yard next door stop to
watch us. House a pinky grey, '70s style like a lot of homes up north.

Wide entrance to a bright living room, comfy sofas. Joan warms up lasagna, calls her husband in Vancouver. I wander out the back-yard before dinner, look for a path down to the ocean. Find a little alcove where I can perch on old stumps. Water so clear the blue, grey, white-gold stones roll out as far as I can see, as if magnified, protected, like they have not moved in centuries. Humps of green islets, inlets, shrouds of deep grey clouds shredding in the deep glow of early evening.

Before bed that night Joan tells me how she knew she didn't want to have kids when she was a teenager and as soon as she could, she got her tubes tied. Never looked back, she says, gives me a beaming smile. These are my people, she says, Kitkatla is my place. We watch the news and go to bed. My room is at the back, a single bed with a floral cover, close to windows out to the wild backyard and, past a thatch of bushes, the sea. It laps in quiet breaths like a baby on its back. How many people have slept on this spot, layers and layers of life beneath me, and all around, the sea drawing in, drawing out.

Next morning Joan calls ahead and there is room for me on the plane but I better hurry. Have you missed a lot of planes? I ask. Oh, yes, if there's a storm, we just hunker in, have dinner with friends, she says, like everyone who lives here. I smile and keep my fears to myself. It seems I have none of Joan's fortitude. We hug goodbye at the gangplank and as I race down to a group waiting for the plane, they nod at me, widen their circle. Dock rolling with the waves, our bodies moving in rhythm. Sky a moody grey and closing in. Billy had to kill his dog last night, a man says to us. He shakes his head and the others are silent. Dog kept running off with the wolves, getting wild, killing cats and chickens. He had to go. The man's cap pulled low over his thick greying hair, sports jacket tight against his thick chest. Two young women with roll-ing suitcases join us. Off to the city? another man says to them, and they answer, Yes, Vancouver. I recognize his voice as the man who introduced us, the Chief of the community. He recognizes me too and we talk of the island, the hikes you can take to the top of the hill outside the village. How he tries to do it every time he comes but he lives in Vancouver so he doesn't always have the time. How he and his wife are raising his granddaughter, his own daughter living on the streets in East Vancouver. How they adore their granddaughter. The plane arrives then, its wings tipped over and rounding in, just like when I arrived the day before.

Cabin Sites, Skeena River

We muster in the loading bay. Seaworthy life jackets, GPS trackers, uploaded maps, data. Weather for October is clear, blazing blue sky, not a whiff of wind, and we're jumping on the day; head to the Skeena before the fall storms make trips like this a misery. Our convoy, Rona and Mary, both eager, dark haired and hardy, pack into my car and we take stock: lunch, water, gloves, toques, extra layers. Hard to know what to expect so we pack more than we need. Never know if the boat will get hung up on a sandbar, stranding us.

It's a short drive to Kitsumkalum to pick up the rest of the crew. Two trucks with wide wheels on the side of the road, grey steel riverboats with slanted windows, looking indestructible, attached and ready to be hauled. Community members standing in the parking lot, nodding at our approach. Looks like we're all here, an Elder, Aaron, says, smile that reaches his eyes. Small man with a gentle manner. The group defers to him, leans in to hear his soft voice. We've been looking forward to this day, he says. He introduces us to members whose families used the camps and cabins we're going to see. They haven't seen for themselves yet, he adds. It's an exciting day, Melissa, one of the members, says, her long dark hair swept off her shoulders, warm smile. David went out yesterday to set up the tie-ins for the boats at each spot, lengths of thick rope for the boats to wait while we wander. Save us some time, Aaron tells us. He will meet us out there. We're bringing an extra boat in case he crashes, Aaron says with a smirk. Launch is forty minutes out, about halfway to Prince Rupert. Just follow the lead truck. He points to the giant black Ford and we pull out behind it.

Skeena threads through sandbars and islands on our left like fingers spread wide, fuelled by hidden currents. Hard granite faces of the Coast Mountains observing us, some topped with glaciers, striated chutes down their sides where avalanches cleared clinging trees. In the winter the road is often closed for controlled explosions dropped by hovering helicopters, and I've heard the rumbles in the distance as I wait in line with the other cars, cold feeling in my stomach. I am so close. Imagining all the frozen water coming down with the weight of concrete.

Sun glares and Rona digs in my purse to find my sunglasses. Born and raised in Terrace, she knows the roads and spurs and what the tops of mountains are like when clouds crowd in. Puffs of clouds drift through the lenses of her own, unthreatening, adding texture to the bare sky. She hands me my glasses, digs in her bag for a snack. This is so amazing to be doing this, Mary says from the back. She is from the Kootenays and new to the area, happy to be coming along. I brought them for their forestry skills, to take pictures and measurements, zero in on where the cabins are on the other side of the Skeena, nestled in moss and rocks. Road hugs the sheer mountains and the Skeena widens, reflects the blue sky. We must be getting closer, Rona says and the lead truck signals left, red flashing bright in all the green bright light. By the time we park and gather our gear, Aaron's boat is launching.

David is waiting for us, steady at the wheel as his boat wavers in the current, cap pulled low on his forehead, weathered yellow rain jacket, orange life vest across his broad shoulders. Tied in so we can climb on the side of the boat and haul ourselves in. Broad smile, we introduce ourselves. I've had this boat for years, he says as he backs out of the launch area while we stagger to our seats, been all over this river, the ocean, everywhere. Broad hull, smoothed steel, it's seen some use. Aaron's boat with the community members behind us. David swings his arm wide to indicate the river, the mountains, all of it, as if in welcoming. We still come here, he says. I was here last weekend, caught lots of coho. He stands behind his wheel, one hand guiding us, the other pointing at peaks and inlets that pass in a moment, speaking with conviction over the waves so we know the names of the places we pass. Brown eyes direct and inquiring, he looks sideways at me, sizing me up. Rona and Mary have barely had time to settle, clinging to the hard ledge.

It is the first time I have been in a riverboat, I think to tell David, try to hurl the words through the air between us but I don't. That I am afraid, a little, but it passes. Sky seems to open up, creating space for our little speck skittling across the waves, glittering in the autumn sun. I sit in front with him, the wide, scratched windows blocking the breeze. We'll head to the cabin right across from here first, he says, and the boat picks up speed, skeins rolling and rippling beneath us like we are flying across it, barely making a mark. Surface of the river like a map he reads. Below us are sandbars, ancient islands that rise only in certain seasons, revealing mysteries old as the mountains that watch us. Deep hollows where salmon rest. Over there, down that river, our families lived and fished, he says, gesturing to a wide mouth of water branching off into a deep valley that beckons, but we keep going. Waterfalls tumble down sheer crevasses, thin streaks of water glistening the cliffs orange and gold and rust.

Here it is, just up ahead, behind those trees on the cliff, and he starts to gear down, pulls up to a narrow ledge for us to hop off. He ties up and we jostle off the boat as it lists and leans, following him up the steep bank. His yellow jacket pops in and out of the moss and thick brush. He's moving fast; I hear his breath deep and quick until he's standing on a mossy trail, hands on his hips, triumphant. Peak of the cabin roof behind him, shrouded by giant cottonwoods. Aaron and his group tie in, I can hear their voices travel up the cliffs, blending in with the constant current, and we converge on the cabin like discovering a temple on a mountain. Place of respite and peace nestled in beauty. Tall and small, that's how we build them, not a lot of room here, David says from the doorway, both hands on the sides, as if holding it up and blocking entry at the same time. We range around him, some below near the river, some on top of the rocky outcrop behind. Built in 1979, he says. Had a stove in here at one time but it rusted so we had to take it out. Families camped at an inlet just over there. Motions with a jerk of his head, somewhere behind him. I'll show you, he says. Inside are two wooden bunks snug along the sides. One wall a kitchen counter. Big bare window looking out over the copse of trees and the spreading Skeena. Floorboards are starting to rot but the roof is good, he adds.

Rona takes out the GPS and we mark its place on the land and take pictures. Kevin, a community member, calls to us from a place behind the cabin and we dive through thick bush to get to the clearing he's standing in. Hydro towers so close we can hear the buzzing, feel it rumble through us. Right-of-way comes close but we're still here, he says, gentle smile. Jumble of rocks and thriving trees, it hasn't been cleared in a while. David suddenly in front of us, he's everywhere, telling us his stories, takes a moment to catch his breath, a pause and a grunt that punctuates his speech, breaks it up like speaking on a hand radio. That mountain behind us here, we used to hunt goat up there after salmon harvest. Voice full of conviction so we will remember, so it will stick with us when we leave.

Off to the next cabin and we know the drill now, hop onto the ledge of the boat while David is easing it out and find a seat quick before he heads into the river and guns it. It's a smooth but fast transition, his reading the water, wide thick hand jimmying the wheel to swerve, straighten us out again. Sky keeps clearing the path for us, moments unfolding to the time of the river. Just over there—David gestures to my right, sheared-off mountain with scrubby alpine and a scraggy top—whale bones were found there years ago, happened after the flood. That's how high the water was, he says. Wonders maybe if he should be telling me this, looks away. That a flood could beach a whale on a mountain, re-arrange ecosystems and drown communities. When people found them, they knew what had happened because they had the stories, he says.

We pull in to the second site, hop and scramble up the steep banks. River is really deep here, David says, good harvesting area. It's why we keep coming back. Cabin here is worse than the last one, smaller, more rotted. Date of 1984 scratched above the door frame. Looks like wolverines have gotten in here, Aaron says as we stare at the chewed-up floor, holes showing the dark earth beneath. Same single beds built along the narrow walls, same window looking out over the cliffs to the swirling Skeena. Forest is denser than in the last spot. Walk out to the hydro lines has us all sweating, trying to find the easiest way, falling into brush and staggering to our feet until the hum of the wires starts in like distant music that we don't notice until we listen, like bees rummaging in flowers. We stand in the overgrown path of steel and wires and stare up at the mountain we can't see but know is hunting grounds. All of us spread out in the sun, relieved to not have to navigate for a few minutes. Wind colder, stronger in the open spaces.

We'll have lunch at the next site, the last one, David says as we head back to the boats. I had already scarfed my sandwich on the swift ride over to cabin two, bits of orange peel flying out of my hands. Rona and Mary said they were starving. Aaron and his son meet us at the boats, not wanting another slog through the bramble. Same gentle smiles to greet us, reflecting stories that coursed through them like a hum. Ride to the third cabin is quiet, all of us winding down, ready for a break. I'm going to drop you off and fish while you have lunch, David says, excited glint in his eye. Was out here on the weekend and caught six coho. He throws out an anchor and a long string of net in the deep current with expert accuracy. Engine cut, boat struggles against the pull, rocking and swaying, David at the helm, eating his lunch with one hand on the wheel.

This is the spot where we want to build a cabin. Can't remember when the last one was here, Aaron says, pulls out a sandwich from his pack, a Thermos of coffee. We had climbed past the rest of the group perched on fallen logs with better views of David fishing, patches of sunlight lighting up their backs, bend in their necks. I don't know what to say so the silence settles like the late afternoon glow around us. He chews slowly, offers me a granola bar. Something about the clearing takes over, fills in the gaps. He tells me he is eighty and was born on the Skeena, at a fishing community that was big in its day. Schools, stores, fish-processing plants. Lived there until the fish numbers slowed, couldn't stay but he still wants to get back there, build a place, show his kids what it was like.

I've seen maps and pictures of the old community, clearings where homes and a boardwalk skirted the beach. Carefully planned rows of streets with names labelled, some of which are swallowed up now. Gone but not forgotten, Aaron says, reading my thoughts. It can always be brought back, just like this place. People we brought with us today can build something for their kids. Look of contentment passes over his face. There are stories that dip and spark in his eyes and I will not know them. He looks over my head at the power lines in full view. Don't have to go scrambling to look for the right-of-way here, he adds, it's right on top of us. I can hear the submerged voices, all that energy in a torrent racing to the port of Prince Rupert. Won't need to measure the distance here, he says, and gets up to face the river, watch David as he carefully spools in the nets with circling arms, picking up each coho to show us on the beach and we hoot and cheer and he beams and throws them in a cooler he brought with him. He got what he came here for, Aaron says to me as we make our way down to the others.

Fish Camp, Skeena River

Four of us in the company car, rain gear in the hatchback. Friday buffeted with grey clouds, blasts of rain in the early autumn morning. Zane brought a wood carving of a rabbit wrapped in maps of Gitwangak territory. Gitwangak, meaning people of the rabbits, he says, light glinting off his glasses, wisp of white hair beneath his cap. His long body folded in the back seat, cradling the carving like a child. It's a gift, an offering. Can't show up empty handed, we'd be breaking the rules, Sheena says as we get out of the car. She's half Nisga'a, quarter Gitxsan; quiet about the rest. Wide smile breaks out of her sombre face in startling flashes. Skeena mist like a moulting snakeskin lifting past the banks, haunting the trees.

We're going to spend the day at a fish camp. It has been used for hundreds of years, maybe thousands, Lara says. She's the supervisor, youngest of all of us, wearing her authority lightly, a cape to don, to take off. Strawberry-blond hair framing her soft pale face. It was designated an Indian reserve when the Indian agents came through the northwest. Road was still breaking through the bush. Nearby communities like Cedarvale grew a Christian following, their homes hidden from the highway like pale mushrooms. Little church still stands in the cedar. Now the highway rips by the camp, just past a thin strand of trees. Peace breaking up bit by bit. Pocks of steel-grey SUV, rumbling logging trucks blur. Just across the Skeena on crumbling banks, trains blast and chug.

Caravan of company cars, all white, splashes of mud on the side. Twelve of us spill out and scatter to the river edge. Mary, our host, comes out to meet us, hair covered in a wool toque pulled down to her brows. Don't use that outhouse, she calls out to some stragglers in the bush. Over here, she motions and they follow her to camp. Some of us remain by the Skeena. River skein like sin-ew in this spot, languid pool. I haven't seen it like this anywhere else, I say to Zane. Fierce and roving river; when you step in, the current tests you, sees what you're made of. Here it rests, lets the Gitxsan spread nets across its length, yielding its insides.

When the sporties slow down in their boats to fish here, I come out and tell them to keep moving, Mary says. I stand here with my hands on my hips until they go. They don't believe me at first, that I mean business. I came here as a child, played on the banks of the river. My mother and my aunties got in canoes, crossed to the other side to pick berries for the day. Left me with no fear that an animal would get me, she says, or that the river would take me. Left me with no fear. Guess they thought the place would look after me. I'd climb that rock over there, watch for them to come back. She points to a steep outcropping at the edge of the sandy beach. I would wait till I could hear them, then I'd yell.

We are standing in a half–circle around Mary. Some laugh-ing, others with tight smiles. I'm not going to chase you away, Mary says. Hands on her round hips, her face is open. Light enters her dark eyes, stays there, flickers. A senior company representa-tive speaks on behalf of the group, thanking her for the invitation. The honour of being here on Gitxsan territory. She nods, looks at our expectant faces. Gives us the itinerary for the day: coffee and fry bread by the fire, tour of the camp outbuildings, listen to her family members speak about the land. We follow Mary back to the camp, leave the river behind.

This is my sister; here are my brothers, she says, gesturing to her family as we approach a wood dinner table, wide and long enough to fit all of us. Nodding and smiling, they move away from the large black iron camp stove, make room for us. Oldest brother, the House Chief, remains in his chair, waves us closer in. Our bod-ies fill up the awkward spaces, perch on benches by the fire. Our shapes casting shadows. Tarp encloses us, rain pelts, soft sputters. Mary and her sister Louise set out coffee mugs, baskets of bread.

I would stand but I'm tired, the House Chief says in a soft voice. Expectant silence follows, slurps of coffee, rips of bread. Traffic sounds edge out his explanation of why he's weary. But I carry on, he says. Long legs in elegant dress pants, white button shirt, navy wool coat. Carefully trimmed white hair. I became the House Chief when I was still in high school, he says. A House Chief died and they brought me back from Victoria, gave me the name. I've been the Chief for forty years. A lot of deaths in our community. He sighs, keeps going in his even voice. I feel the cadences, slivers and blunt ends of his words sink in.

I grew up in Gitanyow, Mary says. Small village an hour north. I had to be billeted out to a family when I came to Terrace for high school. It was hard, first time I lived away from home. I really wanted to be in a fashion show at school. Even sewed my own outfit. At first I wasn't allowed but then they let me. I wore my own outfit; it was the '70s, so it was crazy bright blue and pink. High boots and a headband. I felt like a queen. She stops, as if catching herself, changes the subject.

After we eat, Mary leads us through camp. Grounds as big as a baseball diamond. Mostly flat, well-worn paths from each cabin to the outdoor kitchen. How many feet have tread here, have run, how many bodies have slept here, have died? Cabins are small, some new with clean windows to peek through. Single plank beds jut from the walls. Wood smooth, honey coloured. Some cabins are old and rotting, sides covered with mildewed tarps. A tree house with plank steps going up. Kids love that, Mary says. They spend all day playing, climbing down, running along the river, going back up. Camp name in wide black lettering flutters on the side of a shed. *Gwax Ts'eliksit.* This is a culture camp, Mary says. Classes come here from university, spend a week. We feed them, they harvest salmon, smoke them. Pick berries, preserve them. If they are good, we tell them stories, she says, big laugh.

Her home is a large square cabin on the riverbank, high ceilings with an old-fashioned cookstove. I had to have it, she says, her broad hands stroking it. Little doors open out to receive food, big doors open for wood like the mouths of hungry birds. Looks complicated, I say, and she laughs. It will be amazing, she says. I fought for that stove, took my whole family to get it through the door and it's not going anywhere. We clump mud on her bare floorboards, voices and laughter ping off the high ceiling, long clear windows. We follow her like pilgrims through each room, hear the story of how many hands it took to nail it all in place.

Note the signs stuck in the sand by the river, she says. We are heading back to the Skeena. Thick black ovoids outline a broad face, red letters claiming Gitxsan land. Some are placed in windows of doors, a reminder. I walked the perimeter of the camp, tried to find the edges where the bush claimed the clearing, where the level ground fringed into wild. How it became this softened and flat after so much use. After so long the skin of the earth thin and tough at once, loved like worn leather.

Mary walks knee deep into the river, behind a small wooden table, wiping the bloody surface with a fishing net. Sharp knife like a sabre to one side. Who wants to go first? A tub of seven coho and sockeye rests on the bank. I raise my hand, step forward into the murky water. Pick a salmon, she says. Skin silvery slippery, eyes just starting to haze. Fish in my hands still a little wobbly but stiffness is starting to set in. That's a coho, solid twenty-pounder, Mary says. Group stands around chatting, some are taking pictures.

I have only killed one thing in my life, I say to Mary. That summer, my first fish, a shiny trout. Middle of Fraser Lake, its lithe body scarring the surface. Not big enough to really fight but big enough to keep. I held it down while my brother removed the hook, goo and scales limp on the tip. Now bonk it, he said, handed me the white club. Try to get it the first time. I hit hard enough to stop the waggling. It's not dead yet, whack it again, he said. It is just the two of us. Waves lapping like gulps. My face shadowed like a death knell, the executioner. I whack it hard and it stops. It's quiet then, the small drama of life and death over. I slip the trout in a bucket but by the time we get to shore the body is stiff, eyes glassy.

Mary hands me the knife, shows me how to hold the salmon upright, slice the head off behind the fins. Knife slides through quick, clots of blood squishing through my hands. Surprised look on her face. We don't say *killing*, she says, keeping her eyes on me, showing me how to hold the tail upright and firm, slice the belly. We don't say *kill*, we say *harvest*. Cut the blood line here, she says, pointing out a thin purple line. Shows me how to use the tip of the knife swift to tear it, then hands me a spoon to scrape out the insides. It felt like killing, I tell her, bending to wash the muck and scales out in the river.

I place the gutted coho back in the bin like it is still alive, that it may survive without a head or tail. That it can keep on swimming. You know how many salmon I have harvested here? How many my family has harvested here for centuries? So many, so many, she says, shaking her head. One day I processed fifty, sixty fish in one day, loaded up the smokehouse for a week. Mary grabs another coho with both hands, smooths its long body. She looks at me as she picks up the knife. All right, who's next? she calls out. Group around her has thinned, dispersed down the beach, back to the fire. Lara walks into the river, picks up a sockeye with expert hands. I am, she says.

After she instructs Lara on how to hold and gut a salmon, Mary grabs the tub handles and leads us to the smokehouse. Long wooden slats, thin grey beams draped with silver bodies, sliced thin. Different sizes, like branches, with knots and bends. Smoke drifts from the centre. I start the fire in the morning, watch it all day and into the night, she says. Dark inside, fire snatching the air. All the bodies crowded in, silence around her booming voice. We are reverent, bowed in the gloom. Scraps of light creeping through openings in the roof. Long time to spend in a shadowy place, Lara says and Mary laughs. It takes a long time all right. She leads us back out into the grey air. Autumn, the time of year when the sky and the river feel like one. Like we are under water mostly, then come up for air. With a sharp knife, she slices slivers of salmon, rich and red, into our mouths.

Zane comes back from the car with his hands behind his back. Mary, you told me that you had a carving of a rabbit at the gates of the camp and that it was stolen. In appreciation of this day, what you have shared and showed us, thank you. Tall and gentle, he hands her the rabbit wrapped in the maps; they rustle like dry leaves as she unwraps it, holds it up to the group. Small and erect with big ears, carved in smooth strokes. This time it will go in the bush, she says, with a stone frog, wooden eagle, hidden by the leaves and moss. Only I will know that it is there.

Before we go, we gather at the river. Some of us wade in. Skeena grazes the tops of my boots. Skeena's rising, Mary says to us. This morning my tub was on the sand, now it might drift away. Standing in the river, processing fish clears your soul, she says. Ripples take the guts and blood away, go through your own insides, the mess of you, and you're clean when you get back to shore.

I think how water can swallow a person, a village whole, wipe out a generation but for the storytellers who keep the song alive, so that when the flood is over, the story continues. The land and the people return. River flushing out, decades and centuries later, what has been buried, long missing. All the bodies and bones, tree stumps and moose antlers, coming up from the earth with a warning. Instructions for the next time inscribed in our being.

Acknowledgements

Place is prior to all things.
—Aristotle

There are no unsacred places;
there are only sacred places
and desecrated places.
—Wendell Berry

Instructions for a Flood grew out of the last ten years of my experience of place in the wild, beautiful and sometimes dangerous central interior and northwest of British Columbia. I was accompanied by wise professionals, friends and fellow travellers and Indigenous colleagues. I am grateful for their presence and insight on these journeys. Names have been changed to protect identities and pieces have been reviewed by participants and used with permission.

For me, place is a container of everything that has ever happened—glacial lakes, fires, wars, volcanic eruptions—just as our bodies are containers of our lived experience. The land is inscribed by all these events, and we, with our permeable skin and sensibilities, are inscribed by the land. Exploring these areas, and sifting through my experiences, has only reinforced the very real and powerful pull of place, like the moon influencing sea tides and our own internal depths.

I have many people to thank on the long and sometimes arduous task of making these pieces into a book, including Al Rempel, for his encouragement, patience and strong poetic vision. A special thanks to Dr. Daniel Sims of the University of Northern

British Columbia, who generously read my manuscript with a cultural-sensitivity lens and provided thoughtful advice. Dr. Sims has devoted years of research to the impact of the W.A.C. Bennett Dam on the Sekani people and is a member of the Tsay Keh Dene Nation. I am grateful for the care and expertise of these people for bringing this book into being.

I am blessed with the most amazing and loving family and friends that support me on my adventures. They make all things possible.

Portions of this book have been previously published with different titles:
"Fish Camp, Skeena River," *Thimbleberry*, Summer 2019
"Kemess Lake," *The New Quarterly*, Winter 2014
"Lower Road," *The New Quarterly*, Spring 2015
"This Must Be the Place," *Dreamland*, Spring 2014
"Tsay Keh Dene," *Thimbleberry*, Summer 2017

About the Author

Adrienne Fitzpatrick grew up in the north and returned to complete her master's in English at the University of Northern British Columbia; her creative thesis won the John Harris prize for the best in northern fiction. Her fiction and poetry have appeared in *Prairie Fire, CV2, subTerrain, The New Quarterly* and *Thimbleberry*. Her art reviews have appeared in *Border Crossings, C Magazine* and *Canadian Art* and her book reviews in the *British Columbia Review*. She explores the phenomenological experience of place in her work, and her first book, *The Earth Remembers Everything*, is based on her experiences travelling to massacre sites in Europe, Asia and the central interior and northwest coast of BC; it was shortlisted for the 2014 George Ryga Award for Social Awareness in Literature. *Instructions for a Flood* is based on her experiences of living and working with Indigenous Nations in the central interior and northwest of BC.